Extraordinary Swimming for Every Body

a guide to swimming better than you ever imagined.

By Terry Laughlin

Total Immersion, Inc.
New Paltz, NY

ISBN: 1-931009-11-2

Text and concept: Terry Laughlin
Design and Production: Tara Laughlin
Cover Design: Denise Edkins
Cover Photo: Dennis O'Clair
Photos: Fiona, Cari and Tara Laughlin

Published by Total Immersion, Inc.
246 Main Street
New Paltz, NY 12561

For information about Terry Laughlin's books, Total Immersion swim
workshops, visit our website at www.totalimmersion.net or call
800-609-7946 (845-256-9770 from outside the USA). For information
about our Swim Studio, please call (845) 255-4242.

First edition published 2006
Printed in the United States of America

10 9 8 7 6 5 4 3 2 1

Acknowledgments

Thanks are due to many people who have helped in creating this book or who have made it possible for me to focus my attention on it.

To my family – my wife Alice and my daughters Fiona, Cari and Betsy – for allowing me to spend so many hours swimming, teaching, writing and talking with other swimmers. Fiona and Cari are also TI Master Teachers.

To the team at TI HQ in New Paltz, Tara Laughlin, Nancy Reeder, Nancy Lobb, Keith Woodburn, and Angela Dorris for taking great care of our customers and clients and for truly caring about the service we provide.

To Fiona, Cari and Tara who collaborated to take the many pictures illustrating this book.

To Tara for design and layout of the book.

To Denise Edkins, my sister-in-law for additional photography and cover design (this truly has been a family effort.)

To Jeanne Safer for suggesting the title of the book.

And to Bob Wiskera, Bob McAdams and John Carey, stalwarts on the TI Discussion Forum (Bob and Bob are also TI coaches), who reviewed chapters as I wrote them and made many valuable suggestions.

Contents

Introduction:
Why *All of Us* Can Be Extraordinary Swimmers

When I taught my first Total Immersion (TI) swim camp for six adult students in July 1989, I had a rather modest ambition: to do my favorite part of swim coaching – teaching technique – for a few weeks each summer. I focused on adults because younger swimmers had hundreds of camp and clinic options and year-round access to coaching.

I quickly learned that adults presented learning challenges I'd seldom seen while coaching younger swimmers. Kids seemed to pick up skills spontaneously, even when it seemed they were barely paying attention. Adults' self-motivation was refreshing, but their determination often seemed a poor match for common frustrations that included: (1) stubbornly ingrained inefficiencies – I call them "struggling skills" – acquired over decades; (2) discomfort in the water, from simple awkwardness, to deep-seated phobia; (3) stiff joints and underused muscles; (4) skills eroded by decades of neglect; and (5) a lack of kinesthetic awareness (muscle sense).

In retrospect my choice to teach adults turned out to be most fortunate. TI camps and clinics became a "laboratory" for understanding the challenges faced, to one degree or another, by all of us in learning an activity for which evolution has left us ill-prepared. Over time we observed that while the difficulties we face in mastering swimming are almost universal, the solutions are fairly simple.

I was led to those solutions mainly by watching gifted swimmers – those fortunate few with an instinctive grace in the water. I'd been watching gifted swimmers with keen interest – and a measure of envy – since my teens, when I realized I lacked such gifts. While coaching youth and college teams, I devoted myself to discovering what aspects of their talent were "teachable." I. E. What did they do that any swimmer could emulate? While we might not be able to aspire to their long, powerful and supple frames or superhuman aerobic capacity, perhaps we could learn to move in similar ways. I then tried to distill those insights into lessons simple enough for "average" swimmers (like me) to learn from books, videos or in a few hours from a trained instructor.

It gradually occurred to me that most of what we do instinctively in the water – how we *think* we should pull, kick, breathe and position ourselves – reinforces our inherent awkwardness. And that the technique adjustments which proved most dependable in teaching grace and flow were counter-intuitive. In other words, a great deal of what we "know" about swimming is probably mistaken.

Our most fundamental and universal misunderstanding is that swimming is primarily a fitness activity – i.e. that we improve by swimming longer and harder, The experiences of thousands of TI swimmers suggested that the most beneficial time in the water is when you swim with a core purpose of training your nervous system, and let aerobic system training "happen."

The strength of this approach is that you can't help but improve aerobically, simply from spending hours moving through the water with clear purpose. On the other hand, if you focus on "creating heart beats," increasing your yardage total, or trying to outpace the clock, there's no guarantee your nervous system will receive the training it needs. An unexpected bonus was that training with a constant focus on achieving a *connection* with the water eliminates the tedium of "following the black line."

And finally, for the aging swimmer – and doesn't that describe all of us – the most powerful recommendation for technique-based, mindful training is that while aerobic capacity peaks in our 30s, our ability to hone skills is undiminished into our 70s and beyond. As well our capacity for self-awareness and "muscle wisdom" should improve year by year, particularly when we train in a way designed to enhance those qualities. Finally, while physical gifts are of undeniable advantage on land, aquatic skills are far more affected by self-awareness.

So the message here is that, if you lack youth, fitness, strength, or thought you simply weren't "born" to be a good swimmer, the same qualities that make swimming harder than land sports to master also offer the potential to learn to achieve extraordinary grace, flow and satisfaction. In other words: *Extraordinary swimming is possible for every body.*

At the same time *Extraordinary Swimming for Every Body* can also refresh and renew the routines of experienced and accomplished swimmers. Those who swim for health and fitness will learn to make every minute count. Those who swim for speed will find useful and fresh insights on every page. My goal for *Extraordinary Swimming* is to turn every reader into an "expert" who understands how the human body behaves in the water and how to use that information to swim better than you ever dreamed possible.

Extraordinary Swimming is the result of what we've learned while teaching thousands of improvement-minded swimmers of all types – and practicing for countless hours ourselves. Since opening the TI Swim Studio in New Paltz, NY in August 2005, the insights we've gained from teaching have accelerated, because of the opportunity to teach every day, and because the compact space of our Endless Pools allows constant, arms-length observation of our students.

In recent years, dozens of coaches have begun using TI methods with their club, school, college and Masters teams and shared their insights and best practices with each other. Since 2004, we've coached a team of young swimmers here in New Paltz. All of those experiences have contributed to what you'll read in these pages.

And finally, this book has been greatly enriched by the thousands who have adopted the TI way of swimming, particularly those who generously share advice and encouragement on the Discussion Forum at the TI web site. You have helped us learn far more about how to make swimming a more satisfying and fulfilling experience. TI Swimmers currently make up a relatively small vanguard who are swimming the way this book describes. I hope that millions more will join them in the near future.

Extraordinary Swimming for Every Body is divided into three parts:

Chapters 1 through 3 examine the common challenges that face all human swimmers and detail the knowledge, attitudes and habits that will help you achieve success.

Chapters 4 through 10 explain the principles of efficient swimming, how your body and the water interact, and how to apply that knowledge to swim better. While I've covered this material in previous TI books, these chapters present extensive new information.

Individual chapters on **Butterfly, Backstroke, Breaststroke and Freestyle** explain what you should know about each stroke, how to develop its skills, and how to practice it. All of this material is fresh and more comprehensive than anything we have previously produced on the four competitive strokes.

A final chapter on **Training the TI Way** explains how to *train the stroke* to efficiency and consistency. (We will publish a subsequent book – or books – on the physical conditioning aspects of training in 2007 and beyond.)

You can choose to start by going directly to the stroke chapters to plan your pool sessions, while reading the other sections at your leisure. Or work your way from beginning to end. Either way, we promise your laps will be happy ones.

CHAPTER ONE

Transformation: Mind first, then Muscles

Total Immersion is most widely recognized for teaching efficient swimming via step-by-step sequences of skill drills, but I believe the most important distinction between TI and traditional swimming has less to do with your muscles than your mind: We believe swimming should be done as a "practice," much like yoga or tai chi, rather than as a "workout." Our most successful students – including those whose goals were for greater speed or endurance as well as those who swim mainly for health and well-being – have embraced this approach. So before we focus on the physical side of swimming the TI Way, let's take a quick look at the thinking side.

When we train TI coaches, we emphasize that their highest responsibility is not just to teach stroke efficiency, but to share their passion with you. Once you become passionate about swimming, virtually nothing can stop you from realizing your full potential. And the transforming power of passion has been highlighted in two emerging fields of study: *Positive Psychology and Flow.*

Around the time I founded TI, psychologist Martin Seligman began to study the characteristics of people who had the most success in mastering life challenges – he called this "Positive Psychology." In his book, *Learned Optimism*, Seligman wrote that "engagement and the pursuit of meaning are more predictive of life satisfaction" than material wealth, marriage status, spiritual beliefs, or any other factor.

The importance of engagement was also emphasized by Hungarian-born psychologist Mihaly Csikszentmihalyi, whose book *Flow: The Psychology of Optimal Experience* has had a profound influence on my teaching and practice. Csikszentmihalyi, defined Flow as "the state of *total immersion* (my italics) in a task that is challenging yet closely matched to one's abilities." He listed the characteristics of a Flow experience as:

- Involvement in an activity that you value and find intrinsically rewarding;
- Balance between Challenge and Skill: the activity is neither too easy nor too difficult;
- Intense concentration on clear goals;
- Direct and immediate feedback;
- A sense of personal control.

In the chapters that follow, besides showing the most effective way to develop your strokes, I will also show you how to practice so the components of Flow increase along with your skill. From now on, rather than train for endurance or speed, swim to experience Flow...and by doing so learn that speed and endurance improve almost effortlessly. After all, what could be more appropriate in swimming than Flow?

Powerful Attitudes

Since 1989, TI has taught tens of thousands of swimmers; most are not only swimming better, they now love swimming and expect to continue improving and learning for life. Many possess attitudes I hope this book will help you develop:

1. Passion for Swimming. Once you become passionate about swimming and understand swimming's unique capacity to become a path to personal growth, you'll practice it with an engagement and motivation that will continually renew your passion.

2. Understanding. From teaching thousands of formerly struggling swimmers, we've discovered simple explanations and practical solutions for the most common frustrations of swimming. I'm not suggesting that swimming well is easy; after 40 years I'm still learning important lessons. But the confidence of knowing you are practicing sound principles is invaluable.

3. Self-Awareness. A fundamental principle of the TI program is *mindfulness*, of becoming immersed in how you interact with, and experience, the water. In the beginning your awareness will be of where are your head, limbs, torso, etc. Later you'll shift to subtler cues – the sound your hand makes as it enters the water or how you use it to "trap" water. This habit of attention will lead to Flow and Continuous Improvement.

Powerful Experience

By making time to read this book, you are deciding to take personal control over your swimming. To understand how things work is to gain control over them. The first part of the book explains how the human body works in water and the second part outlines lessons that will improve your ability to use your body intelligently and effectively. In both, we'll ask you to critically examine your inbred instincts about swimming because though we may have evolved from aquatic creatures, we've lost our aquatic instincts. But it is possible to relearn aquatic awareness with the right training. And when you do, you'll be excited by what happens next.

If you were fortunate to have been born with the innate "water sense" of Olympic champions, you would instinctively understand that stroking smoothly is more effective than thrashing indiscriminately. But our experience with thousands of students suggests that perhaps one person in a hundred has the native ability to swim fluently without *unlearning* bad habits. The rest of us practice what I call "struggling skills." And the more you train, the more permanent you make your struggling skills. Years ago, we realized we were teaching people to do things they would never do on their own, but these counter-intuitive techniques were replacing clumsy "human-swimming" movements with graceful "fishlike" movement.

Swimming with "fishlike" grace is a subtle and elusive skill, best learned through a series of relatively simple mini-skills. Mastering the basics can make such a powerful difference that within your first hour or two of TI Practice, you should be flowing through the water with more ease and comfort than ever before.

The key is having the patience to master the *art* of swimming, before you train for it as a *sport*. Take as long as necessary to become completely comfortable with the initial drills in each stroke progression. Every swimmer who takes the time to master each step before progressing to the next will soon swim with unprecedented comfort, which will be an invaluable foundation as you progress to more advanced drills. We've seen it happen with thousands of swimmers, regardless of their age, strength, physical condition, or level of coordination. I hope you'll decide to join them.

CHAPTER TWO

From Frustration to Continuous Improvement

Kaizen is a Japanese word that means "Continuous Improvement." It was first adopted into English to describe a way of increasing the efficiency of manufacturing processes through statistical analysis. When I first heard it, I thought it should apply equally to swimming. As I'll explain here, every swimmer ought to be able to increase their skill and mastery continuously, if gradually, for 30 or more years. But frustration and stagnation are more common.

Not improving or working long and hard for relatively little improvement are widespread because swimming isn't encoded into human DNA, as it is in fish and aquatic mammals. Running, because it's a natural human activity, is something most of us learn to do reasonably well by trial and error. In fact the skills for nearly any land-based sport come to us with far greater ease than those for swimming. Swimming at even a rudimentary level takes instruction. To get much beyond that stage, it takes expert instruction, a precious and scarce resource.

Those who receive no, or ineffective, instruction can make up a catalog of common frustrations:
- Athletes who can run effortlessly for miles find themselves panting after a single lap in the pool, and wonder if swimming requires its own special form of fitness. (It doesn't.)
- Experienced swimmers, who can swim a mile or more, commonly train for years with little or no improvement. When they seek help, they often receive advice that is hard to fol-

low or produces little change. Over several years, a dedicated swimmer may receive dozens of "stroke tips" from well-meaning fellow swimmers. Even when these tips produce some improvement, it's often fleeting and hard to reproduce.

- Too many of those who swim well enough to join a team come to believe that swimming isn't supposed to be fun. When coaches believe that only grueling and exhausting training will enable you to swim your best, swimming changes from carefree play into tedious repetition with the result that most competitive swimmers "retire" while still in their teens then, as adults, prefer anything but swimming, for exercise. I've experienced all of these myself.

During my adolescent summers I would play ball each morning, and "play swimming" at the village pool each afternoon. By exploring what I could do in water that wasn't possible on land – and happily oblivious to whether I was getting in shape or going fast – I learned spontaneously how to move through water. I wasn't efficient, but being comfortable and confident in the water is invaluable.

At 15 I joined my first swim team and began to focus on swimming faster and harder. While I loved training and racing – as I still do 40 years later – I gradually lost touch with the simple pleasure of carefree play in the water. And my time of improvement was relatively fleeting: I progressed from age 15 to 18, but – despite working harder than any of my teammates – stagnated, then regressed from age 19 on. After pushing through pain barriers and thousands of laps, by age 21, swimming had become a chore, and I too "retired" as an athlete to begin coaching.

But after I began coaching at 21, I began to see ways to make swimming pleasurable and satisfying again, without compromising endurance or speed. In my late 30s, after 17 years away from traditional training and without a coach to assign exhausting repeat sets, I began training again, for Masters swimming. By focusing on doing what felt right, rather than on making myself tired, I began progressing again and have experienced Kaizen – Continuous Improvement – ever since.

At age 55, my swim practice is always focused on feeling *connected* to the water. And, to my excitement, I'm swimming better than ever. Never before has swimming been this satisfying. Every pool session is enjoyable and interesting. Every lap feels smoother, more purposeful, more *harmonious* than the millions of yards I ground out in college. I have seen my stroke efficiency, and my awareness of how to work *with* the water, grow without interruption for over 20 years.

Swimming is unique among all sports in the opportunity it offers to defy age and continue improving for decade after decade. Moving a human body through water requires so many subtle skills that the combination of time, clear focus, and mindfulness can add more to your Mastery than whatever age may subtract from your physical capacity. Because I hope to continue learning and improving into my 80s, I swim every lap in a way calculated to produce the greatest awareness.

My experience of burning out on *longer-and-harder* and experiencing renewal on *relaxed-and-fluent* has now been shared by thousands and helps explain why Total Immersion has inspired such passion. By simplifying the route to efficient swimming, we've made it possible for swimmers to pursue the goal of *Kaizen* (Continuous Improvement) Swimming. Finally, we've replaced mindless workouts with thoughtful *practice*. So let's examine the reasons why swimming has frustrated you up to now, then learn the common-sense solutions that can put you on the path to Continuous Improvement.

CHAPTER THREE

Smart Solutions to Common Swimming Challenges

If you've found swimming a challenge, it may comfort you – just a little – to learn you're like most everyone else. Virtually everyone works too hard for too little reward, and few swimmers are truly satisfied with how they feel in the water. That's because of what I call the Universal Human-Swimming Problem or UHSP. Humans are "programmed" to swim inefficiently and traditional instruction mainly reinforces our instinctive errors. Most humans are too busy simply surviving to ever dream of grace, efficiency or real pleasure. Here's why "survival swimming" is so common:

1. You think you're sinking.

And you are. Because the only part of your body that floats is your lungs, the human body's natural position is 95 percent underwater. Gravity drags your hips down, while buoyancy pushes your chest up. You're not really sinking, at least not in the sense that you're likely to go to the bottom. But, because your brain interprets this as sinking, your instincts take over and you do whatever it takes to stay afloat, using *survival strokes* that consume copious amounts of energy but are almost completely ineffective for propulsion.

Through years of training, persistent swimmers can learn to swim greater distances, but in most cases are still wasting 95 percent of their energy because: (1) they spend more energy fighting their sinking tendencies than moving forward; and (2) the "struggling skills" imprinted during their earliest laps are still burned into muscle memory.

2. Water is a wall.

Think about how "thick" the air feels when you hold your arm out a car window even at low speeds. Well, because water is nearly 1000 times denser than air, water drag is *huge* even at slow speeds. To understand just how much of a wall the water is, try walking – or, better yet, running – next time you're in the pool. An unbalanced body and survival-stroking combines with the force of drag to create a "perfect storm" of wasted energy. And energy waste, not lack of fitness, is why you tire so quickly.

3. Water is hard to hold.

While the water resists your body so implacably, it just swirls away when you try to grip it. In addition, your hand is tiny compared to the body it's trying to propel. And finally, even when you do it *perfectly*, pushing water back is an inefficient form of propulsion – did you ever hear of a paddlewheel steamboat breaking a speed record? Compared to running, where you push off solid ground and move through "thin" air, swimming is like trying to run uphill on a sheet of ice.

Traditional swimming instruction mainly reinforces all those inefficiencies: It starts with kicking (and more kicking,) progresses to swinging your arms forward and pulling them back, then prescribes endless laps to "get in shape." But pulling-and-kicking is woefully ineffective in a medium that's highly resistant and offers little traction. And by ignoring your discomfort and awkward body position, conditioning laps simply deepen your struggling skills.

Fortunately, TI offers proven solutions for each of the problems listed above. Here are the innovations that will accelerate your evolution into a Fishlike Swimmer.

Solve the UHSP…with Cleverness, not Brute Force.

Instead of fighting the water, learn to work *with* it by focusing on four sequential skills – Balance, Streamlining, Weight Shifts, and Patient Hands. Instead of using your hands to push water back, you'll use them to (1) improve balance, (2) *pierce* the water, 3) lengthen your bodyline, and (4) "hold your place" in the water. And you'll swim *with* your body rather than dragging it through the water.

1. Master Balance: Turn Survival into a Skill.

For many "struggling" swimmers, the greatest benefit of balance is the transformation of what was a fearful experience into a powerful trust in your own capabilities. While balance is the essential foundation for all skilled movement, learning to *relax into the water* – we sometimes call this "finding your *TI Chi*" – is invaluable for developing swimmers. It breaks the survival-stroking cycle, and frees your arms and legs for more effective use.

Because our natural "specific gravity" leaves 95 percent of our mass submerged, we swim *through* the water, not over it. Rather than fight that sinking feeling, learn to *relax into a horizontal position*. When you do, your legs will rise closer to the surface. Balance actually turns sinking into an *advantage* – there's less drag just below the surface than right at it.

Since your back half is dragging you down, use your front half to counterbalance it. Start by releasing your head's 10-lb. weight and allowing the water to support it. Aligning your head's weight with your spine and extending your arms forward counterbalances your lower body, helping you achieve a horizontal position without kicking and greatly reducing drag. Releasing your head will also relax your neck and shoulders.

And once you relax into the water and feel its reassuring support, then you gain the presence of mind – and the leisure – to use your arms and legs to maximum advantage.

2. *Pierce* the Water.

Because water is so dense – and you must swim *through* it – the smart way to swim is to slip your body through the smallest possible "sleeve" in the water, by focusing on avoiding drag.

In Freestyle and Backstroke visualize your body as divided down the middle, then shape each half to cut through the water like a torpedo. Rather than focus on pulling and kicking, aim to create *right-side-streamlined* and *left-side-streamlined* positions, with each being as long, balanced and sleek as possible. While your extended arm leads the way, you'll also focus on keeping your torso and legs aligned behind your arm.

In Breaststroke and Butterfly, you move with dolphin-like undulation. In each stroke, you "slither" out from under the water over your back, then slide forward over the water beneath your chest. Use your arms to pierce the surface then slip your head, torso, and legs through that same hole, directing your energy *forward* as you do. The greater distance you can travel just below the surface in each stroke the less resistance you face and the faster you move.

3. Swim *with* your Body Weight.

If you watched Lance Armstrong power up French Alps by standing in his pedals and lunging from side to side, or Tiger Woods drive a golf ball over 1000 feet with a fluid, relaxed swing, you were watching the most economical power source available to humans – the weight shift. Javelin throwers, tennis players, cross-country skiers, boxers and even high jumpers rely on the same power source. So why should swimmers be limited to the relatively modest power of arms and legs when other athletes use the entire body?

In TI Freestyle and Backstroke, as you streamline the right side of your body through the water, your upraised left side is poised to spear forward in the next moment. The energy stored in your "high side" is perfectly positioned for you to add momentum to the force of gravity, releasing impressive power with surprisingly little effort. In TI Breaststroke and Butterfly, rocking your chest and hips produces an accelerating lunge that taps the powerful muscles of the core body. You maximize this power, not by working harder, but through synchronization, landing head, arms and torso forward at the same moment, maximizing momentum by linking all your body mass in one smooth motion.

4. Hold the Water with Patient Hands

When human swimmers pull and kick they consider turbulence an acceptable price for generating power. But when we emphasize streamlining and weight shifts, turbulence is a drag…literally. In TI Swimming, you'll take care to return your arm to the water cleanly – almost softly – to avoid noise, splash and bubbles; calm water allows a firmer grip. Second, extend fully – as if stretching for something just beyond your reach. Third, patiently trap as much water as possible, as firmly as possible, behind your hand. Finally, don't stroke until your hand is stable and your grip firm.

As you patiently establish your grip, your body will be coming into position for the next powerful weight shift. If you stroke too soon, you'll just stir up the water and exhaust yourself needlessly. You may be thinking all this patience will cost you speed. But a streamlined body will hold its speed sufficiently to allow you more time to begin the stroke. Swimming this way will be far less tiring. When you push water back, your arms and shoulders do all the work. Those muscles fatigue quickly. When you focus on spearing, gripping and weight-shifting, you use core muscle, aided by gravity. Those muscles are not only much stronger; they're virtually tireless.

CHAPTER FOUR

How a Longer Stroke Makes a Faster Swimmer

In 1998, Ted Isbell, from Ventura, California, wrote to me, after watching Aaron Peirsol (then 15 years old) in local races for several years: *"I've had many opportunities to watch Aaron because my son is in his age group. Though Aaron is always the fastest swimmer, he consistently takes far fewer strokes than others. During one race, I cupped my eyes to isolate Aaron; he appeared so relaxed you'd think he wasn't even racing. When I shifted to the second swimmer, he appeared to be swimming much harder. As I removed my hands, I was stunned by the lead Aaron had gained, swimming so effortlessly."* In 2002, Peirsol broke the first World Record, in the 200-meter Backstroke and now holds the World Records in the 100 and 200 Backstroke.

Peirsol and other elite swimmers have the rare ability to swim at top speed while looking almost effortless. For years I was convinced their secret was pure talent. Gifted swimmers somehow *just knew* how to remain relaxed at top speed, while the rest of us could only watch enviously. But I have since seen many average swimmers – including some who formerly could barely complete a single lap – become fluid and relaxed. Once you've "broken the code" of efficiency, you can consciously practice the movements that produce it, and, before long, swim better than ever. Perhaps not as fast as an Aaron Peirsol, but as well and as fast as *you* are capable of swimming.

The key is what Ted Isbell noticed when watching Peirsol: a longer stroke. The importance of Stroke Length (SL) has been recognized for decades, yet most swimmers continue to pursue success mainly through sheer sweat. Unfortunately, for those of us without special gifts, training longer and harder usually makes your stroke *shorter*. Hard work, without sufficient care and thought, will often impede a swimmer's progress.

An even more powerful impediment than habit is instinct. Virtually every swimmer swims faster by churning the arms faster. And, for most people, a faster stroke is a prescription for reduced effectiveness and faster fatigue rather than greater speed.

SL: The Mark of Champions

How do we know SL is important? Many times since 1970 researchers have analyzed races at various national and world championships to understand what winners do differently. One characteristic showed up with the greatest consistency: Faster swimmers took fewer strokes than slower swimmers. If these studies had identified superior aerobic capacity as the key to better swimming, the traditional focus on yardage would be justified, but not one study reached that conclusion.

How important is strength? While plenty of athletes pump iron or swim with hand paddles or drag devices, suggesting that strength is the key to speed, researchers have found that World Champions almost always generate less stroking power than lower-ranked swimmers. Because their form is so smooth and streamlined they don't *need* as much power to swim fast. So power training likewise isn't the key. I don't mean to suggest that fitness is unimportant; without it you can't maintain a long, efficient stroke for increasing distances. But at the Olympics, *everyone* is at peak fitness. And the edge enjoyed by medal winners over Olympic also-rans is virtually always a more efficient stroke.

Meanwhile, a growing number of TI coaches at club, school and Masters teams have made SL the central focus of their training and, in every case, are seeing unprecedented improvements.

A Quick Guide to Stroke Length

Stroke Length is one of the least understood terms in swimming (for simplicity, I'll hereafter refer to it as SL, and to Stroke *count* Per Length of the pool as SPL). While swimmers are beginning to catch on that a longer stroke is advantageous, many think you achieve it by reaching farther forward and pushing farther back. This will create a small increase in SL, which is virtually always lost the moment you try to go faster.

The reason SL has little to do with how far you reach forward and push back, is because SL is not how far your hand moves, but *how far your body travels* during each stroke cycle. What you do between strokes affects that more than how you push back: For example, when you swim Breaststroke efficiently some 75 percent of your distance per stroke occurs while you're streamlined and gliding just beneath the surface.

Thus minimizing drag will improve your SL far more than maximizing propulsion. In fact, for inexperienced swimmers, about 90 percent of SL will be determined by how well you avoid drag, and only 10 percent by how well you create propulsion. I've been working on my efficiency for over 17 years. For 12 of those years I focused mainly on minimizing drag, and only began to focus on how I propel in recent years. We'll explain both ways of improving your SL in the next few chapters.

It makes sense that a longer stroke would consume less energy than a shorter one, but in water the efficiency of a longer stroke is especially valuable. First, there's the energy cost of a higher SR. When you double your SR, you burn energy four times faster. Second, a higher SR – and the higher heart rate it brings – hurt your form. As SR and heart rate increase, your stroke grows more ragged and energy cost increases even more. And finally, you create far more turbulence when stroking at a high rate.

How Stroke Length Wins Races

When racing, the primary advantage of a longer stroke is that it allows you to make choices not available to inefficient swimmers – particularly near the end of the race as everyone is tiring, and differences in efficiency become magnified. In the studies I mentioned, the researchers observed that faster swimmers usually had small advantages in SL in the first half of their races. These became *large* advantages in the final laps. At the Olympics, when all the world's top swimmers are racing, virtually all races are decided in the second half. Late in the race, successful swimmers were able to increase their speed *and* maintain (and in some cases actually increase) the SL they started with. Slower swimmers stroked faster, but shorter, as they strained to stay with their more efficient rivals.

When you start a race with a longer stroke, you'll swim the early stages at a lower heart rate. The less efficient swimmer has to work harder simply to have a chance of staying near the more efficient swimmer cruising smoothly in the next lane. And because both HR and SR are limited, the efficient swimmer has more room to increase both when the race is on the line.

Those of you who race have probably had the unpleasant experience of watching helplessly as a swimmer in an adjacent lane pulls away – and concluded you needed to train harder. I spent many years being left behind by other swimmers, before changing my fortunes by decreasing my stroke count, rather than increasing my lap count. From 1996 to 1999, I coached the sprinters at USMA-West Point with this strategy – fewer strokes rather than more laps – and all swam faster than ever before.

If you'd like to take control of your swimming – starting each race with a plan for using the optimal SPL for each stage, then calmly executing your plan to decide races on your own terms – you can make this a reality by making SPL a primary focus of your training.

CHAPTER FIVE

How to Achieve Your Optimal Stroke Length

Although most swimmers are unaware of it, virtually everything that happens in training influences your SL in some way – how far you swim between rest intervals, how long you rest before starting again, and how fast you swim. In conventional workouts, those choices are decided by their effect on "energy system development." In TI practice, they will mainly be determined by how they influence your efficiency. We don't ignore conditioning effects, but never focus on them exclusively.

The key difference between TI practice and conventional workouts is constant awareness of SL. As you develop new skills, monitoring your SPL alerts you to when old habits compromise your efficiency. To begin training the TI Way, (1) start counting your strokes, and (2) use that information to guide your choices about how far or fast to swim, how much rest to take, etc. TI swimmers decide how many strokes they will take each time they start a lap. They may not hit their target count every time, but even when they miss, they learn something useful, then use that awareness to increase their consistency and control with each practice lap.

The greatest value of stroke counting is that it provides a constant measure of your efficiency. When you realize you've lost efficiency, you can reduce distance or speed, increase your rest interval, or perhaps swim more *silently* or relax more. How to count? I count as each hand enters on Freestyle and Backstroke, and as my hands extend forward in Breaststroke and

Butterfly. What's most important is that you're no longer swimming blind. Swimming without a stroke count is like driving without a speedometer. Indeed, for 99 percent of all swimmers, knowing your stroke count is more important than knowing your time.

What's the "right" count?

There is no single SPL that's "right" in all circumstances. A shorter swimmer will generally take more strokes than a taller one. Your SPL for a 400 will be higher than for a 100, or higher when swimming a 50 in 40 seconds, than in 45 seconds. But counting strokes regularly gives you the information to make strategic choices: If your count increases significantly as you go farther or faster, you can judge whether that was the best approach, or set a goal of doing it more efficiently next time. Every lap that includes stroke counting automatically gains in awareness and purpose.

Your goal is not to achieve a single "best" count, but to learn the range of counts at which you can swim effectively. This range will vary by stroke. In Freestyle, my range in a 25-yard pool is usually between 11 and 15 SPL (12 to 16 SPL in a 25-meter pool and 30 to 40 SPL in a 50-meter pool.). My 25-yard SPL range for the other strokes are approximately 12 to 16 SPL for Backstroke, and approximately 6 to 8 SPL for Breaststroke; in Butterfly I use just two counts: 8 SPL when swimming slowly and mindfully, and 9 SPL when swimming more briskly. Counts are lower – and ranges narrower – in Breaststroke and Butterfly because you stroke with both arms simultaneously. In Butterfly stroke rhythm is so important that it's difficult to change SL much and still remain efficient. We'll explore this further in the chapters devoted to each stroke.

Is a low count always better?

I've often seen swimmers who have been working on their SL, swimming with an impressively low SPL – let's say 12 strokes for 25 meters of freestyle – but a thoroughly inefficient style. They're actually working harder at the lower count than they would if they allowed a few more strokes, because they strain so much to do it, usually with a lunging, overkicking, non-rhythmic style. It takes more effort to maintain a stroke count that's too low for your skill level.

Your object is to find the *optimal* rather than *minimum* SPL. Your lowest SPL should be fluid, effortless, and silent, because the real goal is to minimize energy cost, not stroke count. By practicing mindfully, your SPL range should improve over time. At age 20, when I focused on harder and faster training, my low count for Freestyle in a 50-meter pool was about 50 strokes. By age 30, it was 40 SPL. At age 40, it had dropped to the low 30s. Recently, at age 55, I swam a relaxed, flowing 50-meter lap in 26 strokes, meaning I've approximately doubled my SL over 35 years. If, on the other hand, you were taking 25 strokes for 25 yards last year, and this year you're trying to maintain 13 SPL you may be exceeding your capacity for adaptation. If you make relaxation your primary goal, increases in efficiency will follow naturally and almost effortlessly. And by the way, if you use my stroke counts as your standard, remember, it's taken me over 30 years to achieve them.

What if a lower count makes me slower?

A lower count probably *will* make you slower...at least initially, but a relentless focus on swimming fast may produce improvement in the short term, but will leave you feeling stale – or worse, injured – before long. Swimming slowly *with a clear purpose* (i.e. not just loafing) builds foundations for long-term improvement and reaching your fullest potential. For instance, the mindful discipline it takes to swim 200 to 800 meters – or an extended set of 100-meter repeats – near your lowest stroke count can be just as challenging as swimming near your highest speed. When trying to maintain 12 strokes per 25 yards for 500 to 1000 yards of freestyle, I have to do every turn, pushoff, breakout, breath and stroke *exactly* right in order to reach each turn with my 12th stroke.

This kind of training provides three invaluable effects: (1) it develops stronger concentration – if you slacken your attention for a moment, you lose efficiency; (2) it imprints effective movement into your nervous system; and (3) when practiced for periods longer than 20 minutes, it also develops the foundations of aerobic fitness. And not just general fitness; it improves circulatory capacity in the muscles that produce *efficient* movement. And as I related in the previous chapter, the ability to maintain SL in the late stages of a race separates winners from losers. It's this type of training that develops the foundation for such enduring efficiency.

As a result of low-speed, low SPL training, I can now swim with a lower SPL and heart rate at every speed than ever before. Five years ago, I couldn't sustain 12 SPL farther than 100 yards; now I can swim up to 1000 yards at 12 SPL. Ten years ago, my average pace for 100-yard Freestyle repeats at 13 SPL was 1:24. Now I can swim that speed at 11 SPL which means my HR at that pace is lower.

Thus, while aging may reduce my aerobic capacity a bit, I've offset that by increasing my efficiency. And because stroke efficiency has a much higher correlation to swimming performance than does aerobic capacity, I'm swimming an open-water mile as fast as I did 30 years ago and am competitive with good swimmers who are 15 to 25 years younger.

How do I use SPL to swim faster?

Once you establish an efficiency foundation, you can choose to take more strokes when you want more speed – and to *practice doing that efficiently.* When I choose to increase my SPL during a training set, I do it with a goal of feeling silky-smooth at each count. An inefficient swimmer can only go faster by going harder. I can choose to increase my speed by raising my stroke count from 13 to 14 or perhaps 15 SPL but with only a moderate increase in effort. I swim faster by changing my stroke timing and coordination, rather than by going harder.

What limits the average swimmer is that they: a) don't take the time to build a base of superior SL; and, b) instinctively stroke faster to swim faster, causing them to c) lose even more efficiency. To sum up: Don't swim blindly – know your stroke count. Practice swimming efficiently at every count in your range. Make *effective* choices about SPL (see box on page 24 for guidance.)

The Bottom Line

Counting strokes is a start, but it's not a magic pill. It *reports* your efficiency lap by lap, but will only *increase* your efficiency up to a point. Steady gains in efficiency come mainly from reducing drag and turbulence. Better balance, a longer bodyline, a sleeker profile, and smoother strokes will come mainly from drills and swimming mindfully with clear focal points. So let's begin learning how to practice that yourself.

Choosing SPL Effectively

Keep the following in mind to make effective choices on stroke count.

Your lowest SPL should be:
  a) Almost effortless
  b) Flowing and quiet
  c) With a relaxed kick

It should, however, require concentration to maintain it for more than a lap or two.

Swimming in the lower half of your SPL range, though slower, still produces benefits:
  a) Makes a longer stroke more of a habit
  b) Helps you stay efficient at higher speeds
  c) Helps you stay efficient for longer distances

When you choose to increase SPL to go faster, it should be:
  a) Something you can do with flow and control
  b) A choice that adds more speed with little additional effort
  c) An exercise in coordination, not in "going harder"

CHAPTER SIX

Slippery is Better Than Powerful

Speaking at a coaching clinic in 1974, the insightful Canadian coach Howard Firby said that most people think of the strokes as having an "arms department" whose job is to *pull* the body along, and a "legs department" whose job is to *push* it along. Consequently, traditional swimming instruction has focused mainly on how to pull and kick; and swimmers train countless hours with pull buoys and hand paddles to strengthen the arms and with kick boards to strengthen the legs. I believe this focus does more to limit a swimmer's progress than aid it. To recap: (1) Stroke Length is the most important factor in how well you swim, and; (2) How well you avoid drag will do more than anything else to improve SL. This chapter will explain how to avoid drag.

In September 1978, I began coaching at a pool with an underwater window. The first time I used it to watch my swimmers train, I noticed something I'd never seen from the deck. As the swimmers pushed off the wall, those who were tightly streamlined fairly *streaked* through the water, looking like fish in an aquarium...until they began swimming. As soon as they began pulling and kicking, they slowed dramatically and appeared to be spending far more energy creating turbulence than on moving forward. I immediately grasped that teaching them to maintain a more streamlined shape *all the way down the pool* would increase their speed more than anything I might teach them about pulling and kicking...or any workout I could devise.

Drag is why no human has swum faster than 5 mph, while fish can swim 10 times faster on far less power. Fish swim underwater and are always streamlined. Humans are handicapped by having to swim mostly on the surface, and by *having* to pull and kick – which, too often, is mainly a good way to churn up the water. Thus even the world's best swimmers – those efficient enough to swim 25 meters of Freestyle in as few as eight or nine strokes – spend over 90 percent of their energy overcoming drag as they swim.

In a medium as "thick" as water, the payoff for reducing drag – even at slow speeds – is enormous. And, because drag increases exponentially with speed, the energy savings from *avoiding drag* also increase exponentially as you go faster.

Water Is a Wall

As I observed from that underwater window, humans can look like fish for a moment or two as we push off, but as soon as we begin stroking, our ever-changing profile is poorly suited for moving through water. The most important distinction between faster and slower swimmers is that fast swimmers maintain a longer, sleeker shape as they stroke. To minimize drag, it helps to understand that it has three distinct forms. Two can be minimized by changes in technique, one by changing your suit.

1. Form drag is caused by the shape of your body. As you swim, you push water in front of you, creating an area of higher pressure. You also leave an area of lower pressure behind you, that effectively sucks you back. (That's why swimmers in training, like Tour de France cyclists and Nascar drivers, like to draft off other swimmers: The low-pressure area trailing the swimmer in front sucks you *forward*.) Form drag increases as the square of your velocity. Thus, twice as fast means *four* times as much form drag.

Because your body's size and shape determine form drag, the best way to minimize it is to slip through the smallest possible "hole" in the water. If you're perfectly streamlined – as in the pushoff – *any* motion with your arms, legs or head will increase form drag. Thus, a single hour devoted to patient, thoughtful focus on how to stay longer and sleeker as you stroke and breathe can pay greater dividends than 100 hours of unexamined training.

In Backstroke and Freestyle, form drag is lowest when your body is aligned, fully extended and rotated with one shoulder clear of the surface – so you should try to maintain that position a bit longer in each stroke.

In Breaststroke and Butterfly form drag is lowest when you are just below the surface with bodyline extended. In Breaststroke, you should try to maintain that position for about two-thirds of each stroke cycle. In Butterfly, you should hold that position for a moment between strokes.

2. Wave drag consumes astonishing amounts of energy; the bigger the wave, the higher the energy cost. As you double your speed, *eight* times more of your energy is diverted into wave-making. The primary reason why fish – and humans while streamlined underwater – are so much faster is that we don't make waves underwater, so wave drag disappears there. Thus, competitive swimmers try to stay underwater for up to 15 meters (the farthest allowed under the rules) after turns. This is also one reason why shorter swimmers are often more competitive in Breaststroke and Butterfly, which are swum partially underwater. As you'll learn later, being taller – or *swimming* taller – reduces wave drag on the surface so Backstroke and Freestyle are often dominated by taller athletes.

Still, you'll do most of your swimming on the surface and, when you do, the most important things you can do to reduce wave drag are: (1) Keep your bodyline longer for more of each stroke cycle – the longer  a "vessel" is at the waterline, relative to width and draft, the less wave drag it encounters. (2) Stroke more smoothly. Shorter, faster strokes make bigger waves. A longer, less-hurried stroke creates less turbulence, fewer waves, and less wave drag.

3. Surface drag is friction between the water and your skin. No technique can affect it, but you can reduce it by wearing a form-fitting suit. For most of us, a well-fitting lycra or polyester suit is sufficient, but since 2000, high-tech suits of specially designed fabrics that reduce surface drag have become standard in competition. Because this material is more slippery than skin, many competitors wear styles that cover the body from neck to ankles.

Pay Attention to Drag

Besides the drag-minimizing tips noted above, the simplest strategy for slipping more easily through that wall of water is to pay close attention. Every lap you swim. Some suggestions:

1. Feel. Tune in to how you feel the water resist you and practice techniques that reduce that resistance: keeping your head aligned with your spine, spending a bit more time on your side in Freestyle and Backstroke, or streamlined just below the surface in Breaststroke and Butterfly, using your hands to "pierce" the water before stroking, or keeping your feet a bit closer together.

2. Look and Listen. Watch for bubbles in your stroke and try to eliminate them. Also *listen* to your stroke. Anything that makes your swimming louder is evidence of inefficiency. Working on "silent swimming" and "clean water" – not just at slow speeds, but even more importantly as you swim faster (remember, drag increases massively as you swim faster) – is one of the simplest ways to increase your efficiency.

3. Spear. Finish each stroke to the *front* (in traditional thinking, you finish to the rear), and visualize yourself *spearing* through the water, with your hands as the tip of the spear and your torso and legs fitting through the "sleeve" created by your arms.

The Choice is Yours

For a dramatic example of the potential rewards of "slippery swimming," consider this: In June 2002, I swam the Manhattan Island Marathon Swim (MIMS), completing 28.5-miles in 8 hours and 53 minutes. While swimming, I gave 99 percent of my attention to fitting through the smallest hole in the water while minimizing noise and bubbles. Multiplying my finish time by my stroke rate of 49 strokes per minute (recorded at half-hour intervals by my race crew) reveals that it took me about 26,000 strokes to circle Manhattan. Which might seem like a lot until you consider that the other 30 swimmers, by taking about 72 strokes per minute, averaged 38,000 strokes. A focus on minimizing drag enabled me to save about 12,000 strokes – enough to swim almost the entire length of Manhattan again – compared to swimmers who were focused on pulling and kicking. (In June 2006, just two weeks ago as I write this, I completed MIMS again, at an average stroke rate of 53 per minute, in eight hours – which converts to a total of just over 25,000 strokes!)

Like me you have a choice each time you visit the pool. You can spend your time, working on your pull, kick, and aerobic capacity, or you can reduce waves, noise, and your stroke count. By now the smarter choice should be obvious.

CHAPTER SEVEN

"Eliminating" Skills: Start Here

The past few chapters have explained principles of more effective swimming, but to reach your fullest potential, you'll need to develop skills that replace your human-swimming tendencies with a new set of efficient swimming habits. These skills come in two types:

1) **"Eliminating" Skills** minimize drag, conserve momentum and save energy.

2) **"Creating" Skills** connect your most efficient power source – core muscle – to hands that "hold your place" while your body travels past them.

When and how you modify your training to develop these skills is up to you. If you are an accomplished or advanced competitive swimmer, currently in the middle of your racing season, you could begin improving your efficiency by counting strokes, watching for bubbles, listening for splash, and doing drills where you can fit them in, for instance during warmup. If you're between seasons, now is the perfect time to learn new skills. If you're new to swimming or become fatigued after only a lap or two, I recommend you stop "struggling" and begin immediately working on the skills I'll describe below.

Why Eliminating Skills Come First

1. They make more of a difference. At least 70 percent of your potential for increased efficiency comes from reducing drag. The less skilled or experienced you are, the greater the impact of drag reduction. For a novice swimmer, typically 90 percent or more of your improvement will come from improving your body position and alignment.

2. They are easier to learn. You reduce drag mainly with "gross-motor skills," i.e. those that involve large body parts. You maximize propulsion, to a greater extent, with "fine-motor skills" that control how you use your hands. For instance, in Backstroke, it's far easier for you to sense your head position-than how your hand is pitched as it "traps" the water at the beginning of your stroke. While you will improve subtler types of awareness steadily over many years, you can, for instance, get your head properly positioned in 30 minutes or less with the first drill in our Backstroke series. Locking those new positions into muscle memory may take months, but you can make noticeable improvements in your swimming practically hour by hour, as you begin working on Eliminating skills.

3. Balance is a pre-requisite. As we'll see, the first Eliminating skill – Balance – transforms your swimming in invaluable ways. The first thing it affects is your comfort; the second is your sense of control. A calm, undistracted mind, and the ability to make discriminating choices about timing and positioning are two benefits of balance. Both are essential to the subtler awareness required to master Creating Skills.

Balance: The First Skill of Efficient Swimming

Years ago a TI Workshop alumnus emailed me: *"Since the Workshop, I've been swimming twice a day, to ensure I remember how balance feels. Every time I get in, I hope to myself, 'please, please, feel like it did last time.' I can swim at my usual pace, yet feel like I'm just floating along."*

You'd think that a skill with such potential for transformation would be universally taught, but many people mistake the symptoms of poor balance – sinking legs and survival strokes –

for something else. To overcome exhaustion, they do more laps. To fix sinking legs, they do laps with a kickboard, in many cases at the urging of well-meaning coaches and teachers.

Balance is essential because sinking is inevitable. Not sinking to the bottom, but reaching equilibrium with chest up – because our lungs are buoyant – and legs down – because our lower body is not. This happens because we're designed for balance on land. *On land, we* **stand on** *our balance; in the water we* **hang from** *it.*

Our "land brain" is programmed to keep our hips and torso aligned over our feet. If that fails, we fall, often with painful consequences. In water, our bodies still tend toward that vertical position, but the most serious consequence of losing balance is an inefficient stroke, rather than a painful fall. When our legs begin sinking, three things happen, all of which make efficiency impossible:

1. You do whatever it takes to keep from sinking. That greatly increases wave drag and energy consumption.
2. A chest-up, legs-down position shapes you more like a barge than a torpedo, increasing form drag.
3. You lose control. You can't swim tall, or quiet, or patiently establish your grip while trapped in a cycle of survival stroking.

Fixing your Teeter-Totter

When your chest rises and your legs sink it's like a child's teeter-totter, or see-saw, with a big kid at one end and a small one at the other. You can balance the teeter-totter by moving the heavy kid closer to the center and the light kid as close to the end as possible. You balance your body by redistributing weight as well.

Because of body composition, our center of balance isn't at the body's midpoint but higher up, between sternum and navel. If your legs are long or heavily muscled, your center of balance will be higher – just below your sternum – making your lower body more prone to sinking. If you have a longer torso and shorter legs, your center of balance will be closer to your navel, which favors balance. This is also true of most women who have more fat and less muscle in the hips and thighs.

Here's a simple test to gauge your balance tendencies: In hip-deep water, inhale deeply then ask a friend to push you to the bottom, then release you. If your chest rises quickly, with legs rising just a bit more slowly, balance should come fairly easily. If your legs barely leave the bottom, you'll need to practice balance patiently and diligently, but the rewards will be significant. If you remain on the bottom after being released, you'll probably benefit from using fins for Freestyle and Backstroke balance drills, but ought to be able to remove them when you begin Switch drills.

"Sinkers" take note: If you find yourself in the last category, you might consider focusing first on Breaststroke, because a chest-up, hips-down position is a natural part of that stroke, while it causes great discomfort in Freestyle and Backstroke. By starting with Breaststroke skills, you can increase your comfort, and develop more "water sense" before tackling the greater challenge of mastering Freestyle balance.

While I can't promise that balance will come easily, the elements are relatively simple – shift more weight forward of your center of balance, using your head, lungs, and extended arms. In Backstroke and Freestyle, your critical balance will be in a slightly rotated position. You'll achieve this balance by aligning your head and spine and keeping an arm forward of your head for most of each stroke cycle. In Butterfly and Breaststroke, you balance flat on your breast. Also, make sure your head is aligned with your spine and you're leaning on your chest. We'll provide detailed advice in the chapters explaining each stroke.

Swim *Tall*: The Second Skill of Efficient Swimming

Human swimmers use their hands and arms mainly to push water back. Believing that pushing harder and stroking faster moves you faster, they begin pulling as soon as possible. For TI Swimmers, the most important role of the hand and arm is to *lengthen your bodyline*. And the longer you have a hand forward of your head, the greater your potential for speed.

This is due to a law of hydrodynamics familiar to naval architects. The longer a vessel is at the water line – relative to its draft and cross-section – the lower wave drag will be. Thus vessels designed for speed are relatively long, narrow in the beam, and shallow in draft. Rowing shells, which rely entirely on human power, carry those design cues to especially great lengths.

You take advantage of that law of hydrodynamics by swimming *taller*:

1. Fully extend your body line at the completion of each stroke (remember you complete each stroke to the *front*); and...

2. Stay tall for a bit longer in each stroke. The longer you can keep a hand forward in the stroke, the lower your drag and energy cost; and the farther and faster you'll travel. Each stroke cycle has a propulsive phase, during which your body does the work that moves you ahead, and a non-propulsive phase, during which your muscles get a moment's rest. The briefer the working phase, and the longer the resting phase, the lower your heart rate will be. To do this without sacrificing speed, conserve as much momentum as possible by staying tall and sleek during the non-propulsive (resting) phases of the stroke. We'll present more detail about Eliminating Skills in the chapters on each stroke.

CHAPTER EIGHT

Creating Propulsion Part One: Patient Hands

If you had a ticket to the Olympics, and could watch a pool full of the world's best swimmers during the pre-competition warmup, you'd see a visual symphony. Dozens of swimmers circling in the lanes, swimming different strokes and speeds, but with a common signature flow – each pair of arms and legs in harmony with its owner's core body.

To see its opposite, visit your neighborhood pool while the local youth team is training. Here you'll see arms flailing, legs churning, and little harmony with the core body. A key to the difference between elite swimmers and the rest of us was revealed decades ago when the world's most influential coach filmed the world's best swimmer.

In 1970, Indiana University coach Doc Counsilman filmed swimming legend Mark Spitz, with an underwater camera, attaching tiny lights to Spitz's hands to highlight their movements. When he viewed the film, Counsilman was startled to see Spitz's hands exit the water *ahead* of where they'd entered.

This observation that the world's best swimmer didn't push water back, but somehow propelled his body past an "anchored" hand, broke new ground in swimming theory. In this chapter we'll look at how you can swim with far greater efficiency by combining two rare but highly advantageous skills: (1) Make your hands stand still in the water – or more precisely use them to *hold your place in the water;* and (2) Use your core body – and the force of gravity – as your "engine" for propulsion.

The way most of us use our hands – to push water back – compares poorly for three reasons: (1) Our hands are pitifully small compared to the size of the body we ask them to propel; (2) Pushing on a substance as elusive as water is an ineffective means of creating propulsion; and (3) Our arm muscles tire easily when used that way.

On the other hand (pun intended) swimming as Spitz did – *holding* the water with an anchored hand – is efficient, powerful and produces far less fatigue. Still, while Spitz and other elites swim this way naturally, it takes the rest of us considerable patience and discipline to learn to hold water, rather than pull or push it.

In TI Swimming, the core does most of the work and sets the rhythm for your stroke. Your arms and legs take their cues from the core and work in harmony with it. You'll swim faster with less effort because core muscles have far more power and fatigue more slowly. As you've probably experienced, arm and leg muscles can tire inside of 30 seconds at top speed.

When you use the arms to hold your place in the water, and the legs primarily to help trigger core-body weight shifts that provide your swimming power, they become very nearly tireless, compared to how they felt while using them to *pull or push you* through the water.

Patient Hands

While watching several elite level meets in recent years, I began to notice that most of the top freestylers, from 100 to 1500 meters, had in common a remarkably unhurried catch, appearing to have all the time in the world to begin the stroke. Also I saw that, in a remarkable number of cases, the faster the catch, the slower the swim – and the slower the catch, the faster the swim. Without even consulting a stopwatch, I could predict which swimmers in preliminary heats would advance to finals simply by watching for those with the most leisurely catch. I took to calling this technique *Patient Hands*.

When coaches speak of seeing a talented swimmer display the precious quality they call "feel of the water" they're usually describing *Patient Hands*. For many years I thought feel of the water was one of those things – like being taller – most of us could just wish we'd been born with. But after pursuing it intensively for over 30 years – and having my grasp (sorry, two puns in one chapter) improve, slowly but steadily, the entire time – I'm convinced it's a quality that anyone can develop through concerted effort. While it may take dozens of single-minded hours to achieve even a faint sense of it – and years to feel that way while racing – simply searching for it will change your swimming forever. And the effort will help transform you into the kind of "totally immersed" swimmer that I describe in the Introduction.

Besides increasing your efficiency, this stroke change can also virtually eliminate the possibility of shoulder injury. Most rotator cuff injuries result from pulling with too much force when the shoulder is most vulnerable. When your arm is fully extended as you begin your stroke, forces on the shoulder are greatest and your shoulder is in its least stable position. By minimizing force until the shoulder reaches a more stable position, you use the shoulder as it was designed to work best.

This process will also make your thinking about your stroke more focused. A swimming stroke is much like swinging a tennis racket or golf club. Once launched, there's little you can do to affect their course, so it's critical to initiate them correctly. This is a change from previous thinking about strokes, in which you're urged to "push past your hip, accelerate your hand at the end, and brush your thumb against your thigh." When swimming with Patient Hands, you'll give most of your attention to what happens in the first few millimeters of each stroke – and propel more effectively through the rest of the stroke because of it. There are some aspects which occur later in the stroke that are worth giving attention to. We'll cover those in the stroke-specific chapters to follow.

How to Develop a *Patient* Catch

Your goal is to feel the water return a bit of pressure to your relaxed hand and forearm before you stroke. Initially you may not even be sure what you're trying to feel and may swim hopefully for weeks feeling nothing unusual, then suddenly – and perhaps only for a few strokes – sense something has changed. For me it was a moment when the water felt *thick* in a way it never had before. TI Coach Bob Wiskera described this as "like catching moonbeams." I've described it as feeling like "scooping pudding" and coach/writer Cecil Colwin described it as "trapping and wrapping" the water before stroking. However you end up describing it, here are some steps that can help you learn it faster:

1. Balance Here's yet one more reason for focusing on Eliminating before Creating. Unless you're balanced, your hands will be too busy sculling or bracing to stand still and recognize sensations as subtle as those I've described.

2. Fistgloves are the single best tool for learning Patient Hands. Some swimmers call them the anti-paddle because paddles encourage you to use more force, while Fistgloves remove force as an option. The first time I wore them I felt like I was trying to pull with a spaghetti strand. Gradually I found a tenuous grip on the water. After I removed them, my formerly ordinary hands experienced unprecedented sensation, as if Ian Thorpe's hands had been transplanted to my arms. I thought "So *this* is how the water should feel." You can achieve similar awareness, without Fistgloves, by closing your fist and extending your index finger. When you pull too fast or forcefully, you'll feel your finger rushing through the water. With Patient Hands, you'll feel a sense of grip, even with that lone finger.

3. Relax Tense hands can't sense the small variations in water pressure you're looking for. And a "hard" hand provides no better grip on the water than one that's relaxed. Soften your hands
– even allowing your fingers to separate slightly – and you'll feel more water pressure than you have before. And a pleasant sense of relaxation should spread from your hands to your arms, neck and shoulders.

4. Pause Pulling at the water may be a hard habit to break. Instead try to make your hand stand still – just for a moment – after reaching full extension. Then press gently with your hand and forearm – to feel the water return pressure to your hand.
This will help develop a sense of anchoring your hand in place so you can slip your body past it. At some point, some of that old sense of pulling back will return, but for as long as possible strive to feel you are simply holding the water.

5. Go Slow Do everything described above slowly. Do it while drilling and swimming. And when you feel more grip and patience than you've ever sensed before, spend a few hours letting that feeling soak into your skin and bones and brain. And then try one length just slightly faster, to see how much of that sensation is lost. Can you still pause your stroke for a moment? Are your hands still relaxed? Does the water still feel thicker? And can you hold that new speed without feeling that you've begun "pulling?" Until you can swim as easily at the new speed as you did at the previous one, don't go any faster.

CHAPTER NINE

Creating Propulsion Part Two: Swim with your Core

In 1999, I attended a training camp for the USA National Team, to record video of team members as they prepared for the World Championship. I filmed Kristi Kowal, who several weeks later would become World Champion in the 100-meter Breaststroke. Reviewing her video afterward, I saw Kristi stretch her hands far forward, sweep them outside her shoulders and pause them briefly. She then used her abdominal muscles to draw her hips forward to where her hands were anchored, much like a pullup or stomach crunch.

On the video I saw what Doc Counsilman observed of Mark Spitz. As she completed her insweep, her hands were forward of where they began the stroke, and her hips were abreast of the lane marker where her hands began stroking.

This illustrates the primary benefit of anchoring your hand in place – abdominal and torso muscles tirelessly perform work that overtaxes your arm muscles.

I can describe this aspect of creating propulsion quite succinctly. Core power will be a natural outcome of other things you work on in your stroke, especially balance, and because you do it with gross-motor coordination, it's easier to learn and be aware of. I'll give stroke-specific detail in the chapters covering each stroke, but here are key points common to all the strokes.

- **Patience Pays.** Because your torso has much more mass than your arms, it can't move as fast. One reason for emphasizing Patient Hands is that your hands need to wait until your core is in position for a weight shift. If they don't wait, then your arms end up doing the work instead. In Freestyle and Backstroke, hold the extended hand in place until you feel the opposite side of your body poised to fall. In Butterfly and Breaststroke, hold your extended hands forward until your chest has fallen completely and your hips have reached their highest point.

- **Send Energy Forward.** In this new style, gravity will do a lot of the work your arms and legs used to do. But gravity's force is mainly down. To convert that into forward momentum, you need to spear or lunge or land forward with your hands during recovery. Where your focus in the past may have been to send energy toward your feet, in TI Swimming your focus will always be to send it forward. In Freestyle you spear forward with one hand, while holding on with the other. In Backstroke, you accelerate the recovering hand into the water overhead, while the other holds your place in the water. In Breaststroke, you lunge forward with your hands – and in Butterfly land forward *softly* with them – as your chest drives down. Then hold the water there as your hips drive down and move toward them.

- **Swim "Inside Out."** In Human Swimming, when you want to swim faster, you move your arms and legs faster. In TI Swimming, you learn to change speeds in your core and keep arms and legs in tune with how fast your core is moving. Remember, if you accelerate your armstroke, your core won't be able to keep up, and your arms will just get tired faster from having to do all the work themselves. If you speed up your legs…well, your entire body will get more tired with little to show for it. As I suggested in the previous chapter, you can add a little bit of speed while maintaining Patient Hands, by moving your core a little faster. Add speed in small doses, always focused on maintaining the same feeling you had before.

• **What About Your Kick?** A chapter devoted to kicking follows immediately. For now, all I'll say is that the primary role of your legs in TI Swimming is to aid the action of your core body – not (with the exception of Breaststroke) to propel you in any significant way. So your focus with your legs is to integrate your kick with the movement of your core. Details to follow in the stroke-specific chapters.

CHAPTER TEN

Integrated Kicking: Less Work, More Speed

It may not surprise you that I'm not a fan of kickboard training. Though the fastest swimmers in any group also tend to be fastest when using a kickboard – and I've heard reports of world-class swimmers going remarkably fast with one – I'm still skeptical that this proves kickboard sets are an effective use of precious training time. I believe the same talents that allow some athletes to swim faster also allow them to go faster on a kickboard. However, I also believe they might swim just as fast, or faster, without kickboard training. The only way to prove such a thesis is by training without kicking sets to test whether anything is lost from performance, and it takes a rather bold swimmer or coach to discard a training method that is almost universally accepted.

However, some of us have been willing to "risk" training without kickboards. For the past 10 years, I and all the swimmers I've coached have skipped the kicking sets – as have several hundred swimmers on TI-coached teams. And though this sample is rather small, all of us have swum better without kickboard training than we did with it, and no one has ever complained that their legs felt too weak or tired as a result of forgoing the kicking sets.

Most swimmers and coaches do kicking sets because of the Arms Department/Legs Department view of swimming: They believe the legs need to be conditioned and strengthened, and that without kickboard training the legs would be weaker and less fit. That prompts two questions: (1) What does kicking contribute to propulsion, and at what energy cost? and (2) Does kickboard training make your legs stronger and fitter *in a way that's essential to swimming fast?*

Coach Doc Counsilman answered the first question with an experiment in which swimmers were towed at various speeds. At each speed, he measured the tension on the line with the swimmer kicking and with the legs streamlined. The only instance in which kicking decreased tension on the line (i.e. added propulsion) was at slow towing speeds, with the swimmer kicking at maximum effort. But at any speed over 5 feet per second (1:00 per 100 yards) the kick contributed nothing and, at times, actually *increased* drag!

Because swimmers always move faster when using the arms alone, than with legs alone, Counsilman compared the pull and kick to a car with separate front-wheel and rear-wheel drive. If the front wheels turn at 30 mph, but the rear wheels turn at 20 mph, the resultant speed will not be 50 but less than 30, because the rear wheels create drag. The same thing happens when a swimmer overemphasizes the kick. The kick consumes energy and creates drag – more work, less speed.

The energy cost of kicking has also been measured, in studies that compared the oxygen consumption of pulling only, kicking only, and swimming whole-stroke. Each study found that hard kicking greatly increases the energy cost of moving at a given speed. In one study, kicking at a speed of about 60 seconds for 50 yards – moderate speed for any competitive swimmer–used four times as much oxygen as pulling at the same speed.

So the answer to the first question is that hard kicking can add only a modest amount of propulsion to an efficient stroke, while it can add a significant amount of drag and can enormously increase the energy cost of whole-stroke swimming. Therefore swimmers should do all they can to maximize the benefit of their kicking while minimizing the work they put into it.

Does kickboard training make your legs stronger?

As with any exercise, kickboard training unquestionably creates some kind of fitness. But you use your legs very differently on a kickboard than when you swim. On a kickboard, your thigh muscles are responsible for propelling you. When you swim, it's best to rely as much as possible on core muscle and to use your thigh muscles mainly to transmit that power to your legs. Conditioning your thigh muscles to propel you – as on a kickboard – is training them to do an energy-wasting, drag-increasing activity. Think of it this way: Kickboard training conditions your legs to *push a kickboard down the pool,* rather than training them to integrate with efficient whole-body movements. Unless you intend to race on kickboards, why train for that activity?

One truth of this is brought home when I compare my experiences around 1970 as a college swimmer with my experiences today as a Masters swimmer. Back then I worked hard on kickboard sets and managed to become fairly fast on them. Yet my legs still fatigued badly in every race I swam and they never contributed to my speed. Today, I'd be painfully slow for 50 yards on a kickboard because I have done no kickboard training in over 10 years. Yet my legs contribute significantly to my speed and never fatigue in training or racing.

The difference is that I was an unbalanced swimmer in college and no amount of kickboard training could condition my legs to the burden my unbalanced body placed on them. Today I'm well balanced and am continually improving my ability to integrate leg drive (from my 2-beat kick) with hip drive and the arm-spearing that propels me past my gripping hand. My legs get all the training they need – aerobic *and* neuromuscular training – because I consciously practice arms/hips/legs coordination on every training repeat.

Right-foot-drive and left-hand-spear synchronize.

The same was true when I coached the sprinters at USMA West Point from 1996 to 1999. While sprinters rely on a strong kick far more than I do as a distance swimmer, they still received all the training they required by using their legs during whole-stroke swimming sets in the same way they would use them while racing – in full coordination with the rest of the body.

And we emphasized coordination over sheer effort constantly. At times, during a sprint set, I would notice someone swimming with a kick that was exceeding, rather than integrating with, overall body movement. In each instance I would instruct them to focus on *blending* the kick with the overall action, rather than trying to drive themselves down the pool with their legs. Without exception, they reported swimming faster but easier with a "well-tuned" kick than with an "intense" kick.

Coordinating your Kick

Though an inefficient kick burns energy and increases drag, an efficient kick will improve your stroke by helping trigger the weight shifts that release core power. The key is to allow your legs to move in the most efficient way while avoiding non-essential movement. A properly timed kick can make your core-body weight shifts far more potent, at relatively little energy cost. To test this, stand with your feet a bit wider than your hips and arms hanging loosely. Keeping your feet flat on the floor, rotate your body right and left, letting your arms swing out freely as you do. You'll feel the relatively rigid, fixed position of your legs impeding your movement and creating tension. This is equivalent to trying *not* to kick – or wearing a pull buoy. Legs held rigidly in place will add tension that impedes free rotation of the body.

Next repeat the movement, but allow your back heel to lift as you swing. You'll find that you rotate at least 30 degrees farther in each direction with less tension. If you also add a gentle push off the rear foot, you'll rotate with even more speed and power. This demonstrates what happens when you link a well-timed, "integrated" kick to core body rotation.

Finally, try the same rotation/swing while fast-stepping in place. Uncoordinated leg movements interfere with the rhythmic, driving momentum you can create when legs and torso move with coordination. This is what I've seen when studying video of unbalanced swimmers. They feel their legs sinking and react by kicking – often frantically. The uncoordinated kick not only fails to correct poor balance, it destroys any possibility of effective body rotation. A balanced swimmer's legs, freed of *having* to kick this way, can learn to coordinate a much more relaxed kick with body movement.

Fly kick helps drive body into streamline.

Breast kick helps drive body into streamline.

As I said above, my main objection to kicking sets isn't whether it's a waste of time, but whether it's possible to make more beneficial use of time otherwise spent splashing back and forth on a kickboard. In the stroke-specific chapters, coming next, I'll suggest ways to use drills and whole-stroke swimming with focal points to improve the coordination of a well-tuned kick with the actions of your core body and arms to produce more power with less effort.

Are you a Visual Learner?

Chances are very good that you are - well over 70%
of the human race learns physical skills faster and
more accurately by watching the skill done correctly.
This section of *Extraordinary Swimming* includes
written descriptions of the drill sequences and stroke
details for each stroke. We have done our best to
make these descriptions vivid and complete, and to
complement them with dozens of photos. However,
this "Cognitive" learning style requires you to convert
words into concepts, then interpret those concepts
with your neuromuscular system without being
able to see yourself as you do.

To put the odds more in your favor, we've created
a series of new DVDs, designed specifically to complement
the descriptions of each stroke contained in this book.
Reviewing these visual aids before pool sessions will
provide a much more accurate sense of how to
master each drill and skill.

To improve your odds even more, practice when you
can with a swim buddy. By watching the DVD together,
then watching each other at the pool, you'll both improve
even faster. In fact you'll not only learn while doing,
and while receiving feedback, you may learn the most
when *giving* feedback to your buddy.

**Find information on these DVDs on page 166
or at www.totalimmersion.net.**

Breaststroke for Every Body

BREASTSTROKE: What You Should Know

Around the world, Breaststroke is the most popular of all strokes, probably because it's the easiest to swim without struggle. So if you find Freestyle difficult at first, begin your development as a swimmer with Breaststroke. This will help increase your confidence and water sense, giving you a head start for mastering the more exacting skills of Freestyle.

I particularly enjoy practicing Breaststroke because: (1) spending more time below the surface than in any other stroke increases my awareness of streamlining my head, arms, torso and legs to avoid drag; and (2) moving both arms and both legs simultaneously gives me a better feeling of applying power to the water effectively.

Breaststroke is well suited for building endurance and your ability to swim farther without stopping, because it allows restful gliding in a balanced and streamlined position. This helps control your heart rate, which is the key to swimming long distances.

And while Breaststroke is great for sustained swimming, it also adapts easily to swimming shorter distances with more speed, while maintaining efficiency. Elite Breaststrokers achieve speeds that few can match when swimming Freestyle – the men's world record for 100-meters and the women's record for 100-yards are both under a minute. The key difference between the relatively few swimmers who can swim at or near those speeds, and most everyone else is that skilled breaststrokers spend most of the stroke cycle tightly streamlined below the surface, while slower breaststrokers remain at the surface. We'll explain how to develop a high-efficiency style suited to long distances and how to swim shorter distances at a faster pace.

Rethinking Breaststroke

Traditional Breaststroke emphasizes pulling with the "arms department" and kicking with the "legs department." In TI Breaststroke, you maximize efficiency by spending as much time as possible streamlined just below the surface. Because drag is far less below the surface, your energy cost is lowest and speed potential greatest when holding a long, sleek bodyline underwater.  Above the water, channel your energy by avoiding too much *lift* as you stroke and breathe. Concentrate on swimming *just over and just under* the surface.

TI Breaststroke has three critical actions, each of which integrate the whole body: Streamline, Accelerate Hips, and Spear. While "natural" Breaststrokers – those born with great ankle, knee and hip flexibility – may have an advantage over the rest of us in kicking, anyone can learn to Streamline, Accelerate and Spear effectively enough to swim Breaststroke well in a race or to eliminate what may have been a liability from our Individual Medley swimming, or just to enjoy efficiency in this stroke.

Streamline

You start and finish each stroke with this action. Drag is least and forward speed greatest when you are traveling – like a Fish – with a streamlined bodyline below the surface. Fortunately the coordination it requires is fairly simple. By concentrating on maintaining a tight, clean bodyline, without excess tension, you can

learn to do this very effectively.
Aim to travel *just below* the surface in a horizontal position, or
angled down at a very slight
angle. To keep your hips at the

same level as your upper body, lean on your chest throughout your
Streamline phase.

Complete the *Streamline*
phase by sweeping your hands
outside your shoulders. Unless
you're sprinting a short distance
– 50 meters or less – take your

time with this. Keep your bodyline – from head to toes – long and
streamlined as you reach forward and out to trap water.

Streamlining is so important that every decision you make
about other parts of the stroke – how wide or deep to pull, how
high to lift while breathing, the timing or size of your kick –
should be based on whether those actions help you return more
quickly to Streamline.

Accelerate Hips

Accelerating Hips adds almost effortless power to all parts of
the stroke. Your abdominal muscles pull your hips forward,
toward your anchored hands, while the accelerating movement
of your hips speeds your hands toward the center and snaps your
feet toward your buttocks.

As your hands reach their widest point and wrap toward the
inside, "crack" your knees (i.e. bend
them slightly.) This shortens your
extended bodyline causing your
hips to accelerate forward – and
helping snap your feet toward your
buttocks. The energy of your hip

movement also helps your hands spin quickly toward the center. Keep your elbows high and wide, then snap them inward to drive your hands back into Streamline.

Spear

The *Spear* converts the power of *Accelerating Hips* into forward speed and drives you into *Streamline.* As your feet snap to your buttocks, turn your toes out to grip the water with your instep. Your hips are positioned  to launch your upper body forward to your next stroke. Your hands have spun together and should be in a "prayer" position with fingertips touching in front of your nose. Drive your entire body forward to spear through a tight hole in the water and into your streamline position just below the surface. Your legs driving back help accelerate your hands and upper body forward through that hole. Coordinating these actions so they work together will pay off significantly in maximizing speed, while minimizing effort.

The *Accelerate Hips* and *Spear* actions should take a fraction of the time that the *Streamline* phase takes, because (1) your body is working during Accelerate Hips and Spear, and resting during Streamline; and (2) you are far better positioned for speed and distance in Streamline.

Head Position and Breathing

In addition to the three key whole-body actions described above, Breathing and the Kick are important enough to merit individual attention. A stable head position is key to coordinating the whole stroke. If your head nods up and down, your body will move up and down excessively. If your head position is stable, your energy and momentum will be directed for-

ward. Breathe with your mouth *barely* clearing the water naturally during insweep, rather than by lifting your chin. Tuck your chin slightly and look at the water just ahead of you, rather than forward. After inhaling, lay your head – as seamlessly as possible – between your arms, so head, arms and torso can all dart forward through a small hole in the surface. Exhale throughout *Streamline*; don't hold your breath.

While some accomplished Breaststrokes may lift higher during the breath, I have had the greatest success in teaching beginning and intermediate swimmers to stay close to the surface. The higher lift takes much more energy and exceptional timing and coordination. The more compact stroke is far easier to execute effectively.

The Kick

In the other strokes, the upper body contributes 60 to 90 percent of propulsion with the legs mainly stabilizing the body or assisting in rotation. In Breaststroke, the legs provide forward thrust and contribute more to propulsion – more especially for "born" breaststrokers, less for the rest of us. But your kick should be powered by core muscle just as your armstroke is. As you *Accelerate Hips*, that movement triggers your feet to move with impressive speed and power.

Streamline. During *Stream-line*, keep your legs high in the water, following your upper body through a tight space, with toes pointed and the soles of your feet turned slightly inward. Keep them streamlined, as your hands sweep outward from Streamline until you begin the insweep.

Recovery. As explained above, *Hip Acceleration*, rather than your hamstring muscles should bring your feet toward your buttocks. Keep your legs and feet inside your body's "shadow" to reduce drag as they come forward. Don't strain to bring your feet higher. Focus more on quickness.

Thrust. Quickly turn toes out to "grab" the water, then drive directly back, just outside the knees, as if jumping into a dancer's toe-point. Finish by closing your feet forcefully, as if "clapping" them. Point your toes and "squeeze all the water from between your legs," to extend yourself into a tight *Streamline*. Lean on your chest while gliding below the surface.

BREASTSTROKE: Build Your Stroke

Because Streamline is the most advantageous position, our primary focus in learning the armstroke, breathing and kick will be on how to do each of those actions so they facilitate returning to Streamline quickly.

Step One: Learn to Hold Your Place in the Water

Our goals are: (1) To keep your hand sweeps compact and quick – helping keep your bodyline long for most of the stroke cycle; (2) To use your hands more to hold your place in the water, than to pull you forward; and (3) To closely integrate stroke and breath.

Drill 1. Practice Hand Sweeps (without breathing)

Learning hand sweeps without breathing helps you establish stable head position.

- Glide on the surface in streamline. Flutter kick gently if necessary to stay horizontal, or just float your legs behind. Keep head and spine aligned.

- Keep your head still as you scull your hands just outside your shoulders – pitching them out slightly as you do. Keep your fingertips far forward.

- Pause a moment at your widest point, then wrap them back together. Lift your elbows slightly as your hands wrap inward – still keeping your hands well forward. Your elbows should rotate in as your hands come together.

- When you return to *Streamline*, glide (or kick gently) until your body feels as stable as when you started, then sweep out again to start the next cycle.
- Practice for 10 to 15 minutes, focusing on gentle, controlled movement and holding the water firmly.

Drill 2. Rehearse the breath

Learn to breathe without extending your chin.

- While crouching in shallow water, raise and lower your head into and above the water without extending your chin.
- Raise just enough to inhale with your chin touching the surface, then lower until your head is almost covered. Move as if wearing a neck brace. Bubble out from your nose as you sink. You'll use the same stable head movement in all Breaststroke drills and swimming.
- Finally practice this with small hand sweeps, still in a crouching position. Sink until your head is nearly covered on the outsweep. Lift until your chin is at the surface on insweep. Keep your head still – i.e. avoid nodding – on both.

Drill 3. Practice Hand Sweeps (with breathing)

Integrate seamless breathing with your hand sweeps.

- Begin by breathing every third or fourth hand sweep, and gradually increase frequency until you breathe on each arm stroke.

- Keep your head neutral and legs streamlined as you sweep out. Pause briefly then wrap your hands inward. The insweep should lift your chin just above the water. Keep looking down and keep your hands where you can see them.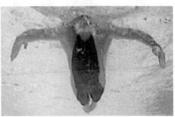
- Fall forward as your hands meet, with your head gently landing between your arms as your hands reach full extension. Avoid waves or splash. Glide or flutter easily until you feel as balanced as before your pull, then begin again.
- Practice: Count how many arm strokes it takes to complete 25 yards, aiming for fewer. Practice as quietly and splash-free as possible, keeping your shoulders near the waterline at all times. Experiment with the following: (1) How wide you can sweep and still feel a strong hold on the water? (2) How long can you pause before spinning your hands inward? (3) Keep all movements unhurried at first, then slightly increase the speed of your insweep.

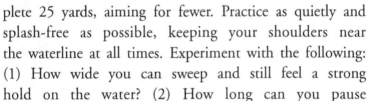

Step Two: Learn to Accelerate your Hips and Spear your Body.

1. Crack your Knees.

- Until now, you should have kept your legs extended throughout the arm sweeps. At this point, allow a slight, natural bend in your knees as you begin the insweep (i.e. just "crack" them), then extend your legs again as you fall forward.
- Focus on lengthening your bodyline as your hands extend forward.
- Practice this as a gentle, subtle movement, without attempting to snap your toes down, to teach yourself timing.
- Breathe with eyes down, chin near the surface and head stable.

2. Snap your Toes.

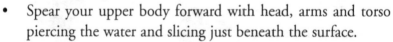

- Add a sharp, toe-snap to the movement practiced above as your hands drive forward. (Note: Just crack the knees; don't bend them.)
- Use the toe-snap to drive your hands forward faster.
- Coordinate so feet and hands reach full extension together.
- Spear your upper body forward with head, arms and torso piercing the water and slicing just beneath the surface.
- Keep breathing and head movement smooth and seamless.

3. Turn out your Toes.

- Replace pointed toes in the exercise above with turned-out toes, but keep movement speed the same.

- Your breaststroke kick should be compact, quick and sharp.
- Focus on driving your body into a streamline just below the surface. You are now swimming whole-stroke breaststroke.

Develop Your Kick

Many swimmers find it difficult to learn the toes-out position for Breaststroke kick. If this is you, you can still practice with the toe-snap version of Breaststroke above, but these exercises can help develop the toes-out kick.

Wall kick.

Do this in vertical position, with arms supported on gutter and hips pressed to wall.

1. Keeping hips and knees against wall, and knees close, lift heels back until they reach your knees. Move slowly keeping feet close together.

2. Pause then turn toes out. Pause again to feel your insteps "trap" the water.

3. Drive feet down and together. Position feet to "hold" the water for as long as possible.

4. Finish by squeezing, pointing toes, and pressing soles together to align feet with legs. Pause again before repeating.

Kick on Back.

Start by gliding on your back with arms at sides or streamlined overhead. Relax back into water until you feel well supported.

1. As above, bend your knees and bring your heels back, keeping your knees below the surface and your feet close together.

2. When your feet are beneath your knees, turn your toes out and thrust back, pushing the water directly back with your  insteps. Your feet should spread slightly as they push back.

3. Finish emphatically, with toes rising to surface, coming together and pointing.

4. Count how many kicks it takes you to complete 25 yards.

Vertical Kick

Cradle a kickboard between your chest and arms to provide flotation. Kick as above but in a vertical position. Concentrate on: (1) Quickness – snap your feet up and drive them down quickly; and (2) Completeness – without compromising quickness, finish each kick by driving your feet to full extension and squeezing them into a line beneath your legs. Do as many kicks as it took to complete 25 yards in the exercise above, then rest.

Kick on Stomach

Practice without a breath first, to imprint neutral head position and emphasize returning head to streamline at completion of each kick. Kick three to four times without breathing. Then either transition to kicking with a breath, or stop to breathe, then start again.

1. Begin in Streamline and keep bodyline long as you "crack" your knees.

2. Hold Streamline and keep head neutral as you turn feet out.

3. As you thrust feet back and snap/streamline them together, feel as if your leg thrust helps drive your head forward into an even tighter alignment.

To include a breath with your kicking practice, add a "mini-pull" in which your hands scull within shoulder width.

1. Start fully streamlined; keep your legs outstretched as you separate your hands and "sneak a peek" forward.

2. "Crack" your knees as your hands turn in. As your heels lift clear your mouth above the water without chin lift. Your hands stay forward of your chin.

3. Streamline again – with head falling between arms – as your feet set for the kick.

4. Concentrate on streamlining head and arms as your feet come together. Feel as if your leg thrust drives your entire body into an even tighter line.

In both forms of kicking, strive to glide farther just below the surface between kicks, leaning on your chest to keep your hips high.

Breaststroke Swimming Illustrated

Keep bodyline long on outsweep.

Keep head still as hands turn in and knees "crack".

Hands stay forward of chin.

Streamline arms and head as feet grab water.

Spear forward as you drive.

Hold Streamline and lean on chest.

BREASTSTROKE: How to Practice

Swimmers develop both Breaststroke and Butterfly best with short repeats and sets. While you might be able to maintain good form during longer distances or sets in Freestyle or Backstroke, that's more difficult in Breaststroke. But that doesn't have to limit your prospects to swim well. Mike Barrowman and Amanda Beard both set 200-meter Breaststroke world records while training with repeats that seldom exceeded 50 meters. They may have swum considerable distances in a course of a set, workout or week, but their Breaststroke training often mixed various drills, pulling or kicking exercises – similar to those described in the Stroke Building section – interspersed with whole-stroke. They were more likely to do 50 Pull – 50 Swim – 50 Kick – 50 Swim – 50 Drill –50 Swim, than 10 x 100 Swim or 5 x 200 Swim.

This form of training has often proven superior because Breaststroke timing and coordination must be so finely tuned that even moderate fatigue – or a moment's loss of attention – can have you imprinting ineffective form in your muscle memory. In the first weeks or months after you begin the program outlined here, I recommend that you do most of your Breaststroke training with the exercises described in the previous section, Here are two ways:

- Do four to eight 25s or 50s of one drill. Stay with it until you feel the coordination described for that drill become consistent. Then do a brief swim set, or move to a different drill.
- Do one to three 25s of a drill, followed by one 25 swimming, focusing on the same point of coordination in both.

Focal Points

Every whole-stroke set should include one of the following: Focal Points, Timing Exercises, Stroke Counting, or Swim Golf. Never swim just for the sake of swimming. Have a clear purpose for every repeat. Here are the Focal Points that work best in Breaststroke:

- Swim with head neutral, always looking down and keeping chin near water.
- Breathe as if wearing a neck brace.
- Be patient on your Outsweep; add energy and speed on your Insweep.
- Move your hands and feet explosively at the moment you "crack" your knees.
- Make your kick as small, quick, and sharp as you can....then h-o-l-d your streamline.
- *Thread the Needle.* Dart cleanly beneath surface through smallest possible hole. Try to spend twice as much time under the surface as above it.
- Sink your chest and feel hips rise as you glide.
- Send energy *forward* at all times. Pull forward, breathe forward, kick forward and land forward .

Timing Exercises

- See your hands reach full extension before your face returns to the water. This helps ensure that your hands return forward without pause.
- Feel as if you *kick your hands forward.* This prohibits a "dead spot" in your kick.
- Practice the following in sequences of 4 x 25 (one 25 for each). (1) Hold your streamline for two counts after your feet close. (2) Hold your streamline for one count after your feet close. (3) Separate your hands at the same instant your feet close. (4) Separate your hands just before your feet close. Repeat this sequence for three to four rounds to learn how to transition smoothly from a longer stroke to a faster one.
- Focus on a constant, uninterrupted "chest-hip-rocking" rhythm. Use a slower rhythm when swimming slowly. To swim faster, undulate your chest and hips faster. Reach a fully-extended body line, no matter how fast your rhythm.

Stroke Counting and Swim Golf

- Using the third timing exercise above, establish a range of 3 to 4 stroke counts per 25. Learn to adjust your timing and rhythm so you can consistently and accurately complete a lap in any count you choose.

- Using the pace clock to check your time, practice descending three to four 25s or 50s at any of those stroke counts. Strive to squeeze as much speed as possible out of the lower counts in your range by making your movements more powerful. For example, if your range for 25 yards is from 6 to 9 strokes, how fast can you learn to swim at 6 or 7 strokes?

- Practice swimming 50s, 75s or 100s, on which you start at a lower stroke count and add one SPL each length. Your goal is to be able to accurately and seamlessly adjust your timing to add speed.

- Compare your Swimming Golf scores (strokes + seconds = score) at each SPL count in your range.

Backstroke for Every Body

BACKSTROKE: What You Should Know

Backstroke and Freestyle are closely related as *Long Axis* strokes, in which the body rotates around the spinal axis. (The *Short Axis* strokes, Breaststroke and Butterfly, are so named because body rotation – actually undulation – is around the hip-to-hip axis.) Both Long Axis strokes share constant balance, drag reduction through spinal alignment and rotation, and propelling via side-to-side weight shifts. Thus improving your Backstroke can often benefit your Freestyle, even without consciously working on it.

Because you swim Backstroke "upside down and backwards," you have to navigate without seeing the line on the bottom or the approaching turn. It also means power and leverage are limited. Thus it's essential to swim with particular finesse and a "slippery" vessel, which should be good for all of your strokes.

For this reason, swimmers who consider themselves primarily Freestylers should practice Backstroke skills as well. Like many triathletes, I'm an endurance swimmer, who races often in Open Water. But when training in the pool I practice some Backstroke nearly every session. I most often do Backstroke drills or whole-stroke as recovery between faster-paced Freestyle sets. Though Backstroke and Freestyle use similar muscles, the movement is reversed – the muscles that were contracting are now lengthening and vice versa – so easy Backstroke can "massage" tired Freestyle muscles.

In addition, the simple act of breathing in Freestyle is a *technique* and many people tense up if they don't have it just right. Backstroke is more relaxing because you can breathe any time you want. But the main reason I practice Backstroke regularly is simply that I enjoy it. No other stroke gives me such a feeling of slipping through the water like an eel. I also enjoy the different skill challenges it presents and what they contribute to my overall "water sense."

To measure my improvement I enter some Masters races each year in Backstroke, which motivates me to practice it with the same level of high purpose that I bring to Freestyle. You can train for Backstroke much like Freestyle, because it's easier to remain efficient on longer sets and repeats than in Short Axis strokes. Thus you can use it effectively to build endurance.

How to Minimize Drag

Learn balance, so you always feel supported by the water. Rotate from side to side, because a sidelying profile is more slippery. And stay "tall" for a bit longer in each stroke cycle.

Relax into the Water. When you feel yourself sinking, you tend to sit up to avoid choking. This causes your hips to sink even more. It also leads to using your arms more for stability than propulsion. The best way to balance is to *relax into the water.* Relax your head back until your ears are submerged and the water touches your goggles and chin, and lean on your shoulder blades until your hips and legs feel light. Olympic champion and world-record holder, Lenny Krayzelberg, always focused on keeping his hips at the surface. When his head was low, he knew his hips would be high.

Rotate from side to side. When you relax into the water and your hipbones rise to the surface, it's much easier to roll from side to side. Rotation reduces drag, while providing the rhythm and power for propulsion. Here are several ways to improve your rotation:

- Keep your head still, as the axis of rotation. Visualize a line from the top of your head, down your spine, to your toes. Rotate that line through the water, like a laser beam.

- Feel each hipbone touch the surface in turn. Lenny Krayzelberg said *"When I swim, I try to feel one hip at the surface, then the other."*

- Clear the water with each shoulder. When stroking with your right arm, you should feel no water resistance behind your left shoulder, and vice versa. Focusing on shoulder rotation will produce different self-awareness than a focus on hip rotation. Both are helpful.

- Always relax back. While focusing on hip or shoulder rotation, keep relaxing your head and shoulder blades back into the water.

Stay long and sleek for as long as possible. In Breaststroke I suggested you spend more time streamlined under the surface, where drag is lowest. In Backstroke drag is

lowest when you're fully extended from fingers to toes, in a slightly rotated position. Try to hold that position for just a bit longer, while patiently trapping water with your hand – your other arm may be a third of the way through recovery before you begin stroking. Then quickly rotate the other hip to the surface…and to your lowest-drag position on the other side.

How to Maximize Propulsion

As you learned in Chapters 6 and 7, the most effective way to create propulsion is to combine a Patient Catch with core-power.

Trap the water. A Patient Catch helps you avoid relying too much on arm muscles. Slice into the water with the narrowest part of your hand and arm (to minimize splash or bubbles), until your hand is submerged with your palm facing the side. Then reach outside for the catch and wrap your hand around the water – i.e. rotate your palm to face your feet – trying to trap water behind your hand. Do this mainly with your hand and wrist; your elbow should bend very little. Keep part of your focus on maintaining a long line from fingers to toes.

Put core power to work. Do this with two focus points:
- Coordinate your stroke so the stroking and recovering arms both pass your shoulders at the same moment. Feel: (1) as if both are "connected" across your shoulder blades so the recovering arm "adds" power to the stroking arm; and (2) that your abdominal and back muscles are working with your arms.
- Focus on rhythmically driving each hipbone to the surface, while maintaining the stroke timing described above. You should feel rhythmic hip-drive powering the stroke, with the power transmitted to your arms by your torso muscles.

Action Cues for your Stroke

Use these word pictures to help you visualize each part of the stroke.

1. Slice. Visualize the outside of your hand and forearm as a knife edge. Drive into the water like a knife into butter. Don't pause at the surface: Drive cleanly in from the high point of your recovery until your hand and shoulder are below your body.

2. Wrap. Reach outside your shoulder as if to touch the lane line, then "wrap your hand around the water" so you can push it toward your feet. Feel the water return pressure to your hand.

3. Wrestle. Rehearse this on the floor: In a slightly side-rotated position with your arm extended and elbow and back of hand resting on the floor, repeatedly rotate your hand off the floor until it passes your shoulder, as in "arm-wrestling." In the water, your hand rotates over the elbow, until the entire inside of your arm faces your feet – feeling firm water pressure.

4. Throw. After the hand passes your elbow, "throw" the water at your feet. Finish with a basketball-dribbling action, then exit the water with the back of your hand leading.

5. Sight. As your hand comes over the top, turn your palm out, and sight up your arm like a rifle barrel as it points up. Your head remains still throughout.

Keep these descriptions in mind during the appropriate drills as you Build Your Stroke, then return to them as Focal Points when practicing whole stroke.

The Kick

While 2-beat kicking (one beat for each armstroke) is common in Freestyle, virtually everyone uses a steady 6-beat kick in Backstroke.

- Your legs should rotate rhythmically with your torso so they face to the right as your right hand goes in, and to the left as your left goes in. Your kick should be light, supple and rhythmic, rather than labored.
- Your kick should ruffle the surface but your knees and feet should not break the surface.
- Kick from the top of your hip, with a long, nearly straight leg. Develop this action with Vertical flutter kicking, holding a board to your chest for buoyancy, and turning a quarter turn to right and left every few seconds. Then use that same action in practicing Active Balance and Streamline Position.

BACKSTROKE: Build Your Stroke

1. Balance Position (Sweet Spot)

Experience comfort, stability and support by relaxing into the water. Learn the right degree of rotation. Create a long, clean bodyline.

- Relax back with face parallel to surface until water wraps around your goggles. Keep the water unruffled and quiet around your face, here and at every step.
- While kicking easily, roll to one side just enough to touch your hip to the surface. Keep your head still and spine aligned as you roll.
- As you rotate each hip to the surface, shape your back like a canoe, with slightly rounded shoulders, to help clear each shoulder from the water.
- Relax into the water and breathe evenly throughout.

Practice tips:

1. At first, kick a full pool length with your right hip at the surface, followed by a full length with the left hip at the surface. Keep your head still and your kick relaxed and compact, feeling as if you're being towed from the top of your head. Keep practicing with concentrated attention to each side until you feel relaxed, "tall," sleek, and stable.

2. Introduce rotation. Kick easily on one side for half a length. Then – without disturbing the water – rotate the other hip to the surface. Continue practicing this way until you feel smooth and balanced on each side and also when you rotate.

3. As your sense of control improves, reduce the pauses. At first you may rotate only once in 25 yards, but eventually rotate 6 or 8 times in one length. If you're just learning Backstroke, allow plenty of time to develop a sense of relaxation and control.

4. If you're a beginning Backstroker, progress to the Streamline Position drill. If you're working on stroke improvement, alternate lengths of Drill and Swim until both have the same feeling of rhythmically rotating your hips to the surface, while your head remains still.

2. Streamline Position

This will teach you a stable and streamlined position from which to start each stroke, eliminate water resistance from recovery, and lead to a clean entry and effective catch.

- While kicking easily in Balance Position (BP) with one hip touching the surface, lift that arm from the water and bring it overhead to a clean entry above your shoulder, while

rotating the other hip to the surface. This is Streamline Position (SP). Pause until you feel balanced and stable. Then stroke that arm to your side, while rotating the original hip to the surface. You're back in BP. Pause until you feel stable and relaxed, then repeat.
- Bring your arm overhead slowly and slice into the water with precision. To avoid over-reach: (1) maintain space between shoulder and ear; (2) face hand/wrist outward on entry; (3) feel your entry is "too wide."
- Then relax into the water and focus on a long, sleek body line with quiet water around your face and your opposite hip at the surface.

Practice tips:

1. You might rotate only once or twice in 25 yards initially, then patiently increase to 5 or 6 rotations per length. Avoid disturbing the water as you rotate.

2. Focus first – possibly for several hours of practice – on stability and a sleek body line. As those imprint, turn your attention, one at a time, to the Awareness Cues listed above: Slice, Wrap, Wrestle and Throw. Focus on one until you're "bored" before shifting to the next.

3. The final step in this drill is to eliminate the pause at your hip – complete the Throw and immediately rotate the other hip to the surface. Keep the pause in SP. It might take 8 or 10 hours of experience with this drill before you can do that well.

4. Beginning Backstrokers should progress next to the Backstroke Switch drill series. More experienced Backstrokers can alternate lengths of Streamline Position and Swim. When your balance and body lines feel good, do a length of Streamline Position on one side, followed by a length of swimming. Think about how your balance and sleekness feel on both drill and swim. Then repeat, starting with Streamline Position on your other side.

Backstroke Switch Drill Series

This series of drills will teach you a slight overlap between recovery and your Patient Catch and stroke and connect your armstroke to core power.

3. Partial Recovery

This teaches you to maintain balance as you begin recovery.

- While kicking gently in SP with one hip at the surface, lift that hand slightly off the water. Relax the hand so it hangs loosely from your wrist.
- Check your balance, then gently return hand to water. Repeat until you can remain comfortable and stable, kicking gently, with your hand suspended slightly above the water. It's essential to be balanced and aligned *before lifting*, then stay that way as you lift.
- Lift progressively higher – while maintaining balance and stability. As you progress to higher positions, practice each until you can maintain it without discomfort for three or more breaths.

4. Reverse Switch

A slight overlap in switch timing between arms will help you minimize drag for slightly longer in your recovery and connect your arms to core body power.

- From SP, while kicking gently, lift your arm as in Partial Recovery then pause.
- If you're comfortable and stable, then switch, moving both hands at the same moment. Flip your hand from palm in to palm out, so hand enters with thumb up.
- Pause in SP on your other side to check comfort and stability. Always wait until you feel stable before lifting your arm again.
- Practice until you feel relaxed and controlled, with an unhurried recovery, quiet water around your face, and no splash on entry.
- The highest skill level in this drill is to eliminate the pause at your hip – complete the Throw and immediately lift your arm to the position you've been practicing to the surface.

Keep the pause in SP. It might take several hours of experience with this drill before you can do that well.

- Stroke Improvers should alternate Drill and Swim repeats each time they master a new skill at this step. Beginning Backstrokers should progress next to the Backstroke Switch drill.

5. Backstroke Switch

Introduce a dynamic recovery-and-entry while remaining balanced, controlled and relaxed.

- Eliminate the mid-recovery pause from the movement above, while keeping the pause at SP.
- Though you recover without pausing, lift your hand as s-l-o-w-l-y as possible while keeping a "patient" hand overhead. Switch when you reach the position where you previously paused. Both hands should then pass your shoulders at the same moment.
- Practice until you can execute an unhurried recovery, keep quiet water around your face, and enter without a splash.
- With an approximate 30-degree overlap between arms, both should feel as if they're drawing power from your core as they pass the shoulders.
- Focus exclusively on the overlap timing until it feels natural, then turn your attention to Slice, Wrap, Wrestle and Throw, focusing on one at a time.

6. Triple Switch

A seamless transition from Switch drills to Whole Stroke

- Begin by kicking gently in SP, then do three rhythmic switches (i.e. your hips never pause). After three switches, pause in SP on other side to reset balance and bodylines. Focus on the following as you practice:

- Remain as relaxed and stable while hips are moving steadily as you are while pausing in SP.
- Keep the patient lead hand and 30-degree overlap you established in preceding drills.
- Maintain quiet water around face and no splash.
- Practice until you feel coordinated and controlled, then progress to – or alternate with – whole stroke.

BACKSTROKE: How to Practice

Drill Practice

Backstroke drills can be used both as stroke tuners and as a way of doing low intensity swimming when fatigued. Drills 1 and 2, BP and SP, offer a way of practicing flutter kicking that – unlike using a kickboard – improves your balance and streamlining. Practicing Drill #3, kicking with an arm slightly lifted, will develop those qualities still more, and Drill #4, Stutter Switch will improve your "dynamic balance."

Backstroke Switch and Triple Switch are drills that you'll probably practice most frequently over the long term. You can practice them in several ways:

- Do four to eight 25s or 50s of Backstroke Switch. Stay with it until the overlap timing feels natural and consistent. When it does, do a brief swim set, trying to feel the same overlap. Or progress practice 50s (25Drill+25Swim), 75s (25Drill+50Swim) or 100s (50Drill+50Swim or 25Drill+ 75Swim). Use the same pattern for Triple Switch and Swim.
- Or do similar progressions of Backstroke Switch, Triple Switch and Swim. Sample patterns: 75 (25Switch+ 25TripleSwitch +25Swim); 100 (25Switch+ 25Swim+25 TripleSwitch +25Swim).

Focal Point Practice

Every length of whole-stroke set should involve concentration on specific Focal Points, Stroke Counting, or Swim Golf and sometimes Focal Points and Stroke Counting or Golf together. If doing a Drill-Swim set, as described above, refer to specific Focal Points on the whole-stroke lengths as well. Never swim just for the sake of swimming. Have a clear purpose for every repeat. Here are the most helpful Focal Points for Backstroke:

- RELAX BACK until your hips and legs feel light.
- Keep quiet water around your face and your head perfectly still.

- Rhythmically rotate each hip to the surface and let your arms follow their rhythm.
- Rhythmically clear each shoulder from the water – no resistance – on each stroke.

- Trap and wrap the water *patiently* and feel *a bit too much overlap* between your arms.
- Focus on having your arms pass each other at the shoulders and feel them connect across your shoulder blades.

- *Slice, Wrap, Wrestle and Throw* – but only one at a time.

Stroke Counting and Swim Golf

- Establish a range of 3 to 4 SPL counts, which ought to be fairly close to your SPL for Freestyle. Learn to adjust your timing and rhythm so you can consistently and accurately complete a lap in any SPL you choose.
- Using the pace clock to check your time, practice descending three to four 25s or 50s at one SPL. Strive to squeeze as much speed as possible out of the lower counts in your range by making your movements more powerful. For example, if your SPL range for 25 yards is from 14 to 17

strokes, how fast can you learn to swim at 14 or 15 strokes?

- Practice swimming 50s, 75s or 100s, on which you start at a lower count and add one SPL each length. Your goal is to feel smooth at every SPL and to gain "easy speed" each time you raise your SPL.
- Compare your Swimming Golf scores (strokes + seconds = score) at each SPL count in your range.

Use Fistgloves.

I feel I have probably benefited more from Fistglove practice in Backstroke than any other stroke, particularly increased effectiveness in Wrap, Wrestle and Throw. After practicing drills or whole-stroke for 20 or more minutes, I feel as if I can work *with* the water like an Olympian. That allows me to begin each stroke with more care and helps increase my Stroke Length. And because gripping power is reduced, I'm encouraged even more to rely on rhythmic hip drive, which keeps me more relaxed at all speeds. If you regularly use Fistgloves for the first half of any of the drills, Focal Points or Stroke Counting exercises suggested above, you'll progress more rapidly than otherwise.

Swimming for Distance

Backstroke is especially well suited to the longer sets and longer swims that many people do with the Freestyle stroke to build fitness and endurance. When you have great balance, Backstroke is so relaxing and can be done with such ease that it should be just as easy to swim a set of 20 x 100, or a continuous hour, as with an efficient Freestyle. However, if you do swim long distances, always have a Focal Point in mind, and check your SPL from time to time.

Butterfly for Every Body

Butterfly: What You Should Know

Butterfly (sometimes abbreviated as "Fly") has a reputation as the most "grueling" stroke. But that reputation has come mainly because so many people swim Butter*Struggle*. When swum with relaxation and economy, Butterfly is beautiful to watch and satisfying to swim. I learned this firsthand only after struggling with it for 40 years.

Though I've coached world-ranked butterfliers, the teaching methods that made those gifted swimmers successful had little effect on me. One or two lengths of a 25-yard pool always left me exhausted. At age 50, I finally concluded that my body just wasn't meant to learn Fly and gave myself a "middle-age exemption" from swimming it. For several years I didn't attempt a single stroke.

But, while studying video of world-record holder Michael Phelps, frame by frame, I noticed subtleties that had eluded me before. Excited by this, I modified stroke drills I had used for decades previously. After just a few hours of practice, I began to feel as if I could master this challenging stroke. Before long, I could swim 8, 12 and then 16 lengths of a 25-yard pool (resting briefly between laps) with little fatigue.

I'll never be a threat to Michael Phelps, but after decades of frustration, I'm so excited about this midlife breakthrough that I plan to enter the 200 Fly in a Masters meet – and aim to win a medal when I do. If you have never swum Butterfly, or last did so in high school, and think you may now be too old to swim it, keep in mind that I mastered Butterfly for the first time at age 55 and have since seen swimmers in their 60s and 70s learn it in a matter of hours.

Mastering Butterfly will heighten your awareness of skills important in every stroke: streamlining, holding water, core-powered movement, sensitivity to the water, and rhythm. Those who learn to swim Fly skillfully are also highly likely to swim the other strokes well; this is less often the case for those who have mastered Freestyle, Backstroke or Breaststroke.

With the TI approach, *anyone* can learn to swim an effortless 25 yards or meters – then build from there to longer distances with surprising ease. And it will also give you the foundation to swim with greater speed and power. Regardless of whether your goal is to swim with ease or speed, the first step is to stop wasting energy. Here are the three energy-wasters that make ButterStruggle so exhausting:

• **Pulling and Kicking:** ButterStrugglers use the arms to pull back and flail forward and the legs to keep the hips afloat. Efficient flyers use integrated whole-body movement instead of pulling and kicking.

• **Climbing Out:** Gravity is such an unforgiving force that it makes more sense to *use* it than fight it. Butterstrugglers try to climb out of the water as they swim. Efficient flyers *hug the surface* as they come over the water, then *use* gravity by letting a sinking chest lift the hips to the surface.

• **OverPowering:** *Butterfly is a rhythm stroke, not a power stroke.* Those who swim it best and fastest are more likely to be supple and graceful than powerful. The key rhythm in Fly is a chest-hip-rocking rhythm. Focus on keeping this rhythm consistent in drills and whole-stroke.

When you change your *thinking* about Butterfly, you'll be surprised at how much easier *swimming* it can be.

How to Maximize Relaxation and Minimize Drag

Save energy by streamlining your bodyline.

Stay "tall." In Butterfly, drag is lowest when you're stretched out and streamlined just below the surface. In Fly, to stay "tall" for more of each stroke cycle, be *very patient* when your hands are  forward, and *very quick* from the moment they start moving.
Streamline. When you land, pierce the water and streamline. Concentrate on keeping your legs long until your chest sinks completely, then just "crack" your knees (bend them as slightly as possible) to initiate the next stroke. And kick "quietly" – no noise or splash from your feet, whether drilling or swimming.

How to Create Propulsion

A Patient Catch and power from the core get more done with less effort.

Just hold on. Rather than push water back, *anchor* your hands, slide your chest over your anchored hands and quickly release the water. Your arm muscles need only "hold your place" while powerful torso muscles do the harder work of accelerating you forward.

Swim *forward.* Here and in the drill section, you'll see the direction "forward" repeated frequently – for hands, head, chest, and hips. Channel your energy forward at all times and as you return to the water, land *cleanly,* pierce the water and streamline to conserve momentum.

One Fluent, Effective Stroke

Here is a moment-by-moment sequence of what happens in an efficient Comfort Fly stroke.

Land... *Forward...Softly.* Land your head before your hands, keeping your head neutral (i.e. don't thrust your chin down.) Land with arms wide enough to sink easily between them. Leave your forearms near the surface.

Sink. *Being patient here puts you in a power position; it also keeps your bodyline longer for a bit more of the stroke cycle.* While your forearms stay near the surface, let your chest just sink until you feel your hips are higher than your chest. Spread your hands and elbows slightly to engage your upper back muscles and trap the water.

Hold. As your sinking chest lifts your hips, it also creates pressure on your hands that provides traction. Pause your kick a moment – keeping your legs streamlined near the surface – to feel the stored power in your midsection. Then pull *softly enough to hold your place.*

Slide. After keeping your legs high and streamlined, "crack" your knees and use arms and core muscle to bring your chest over your hands. Your hands sweep inward to stay in place – think of a keyhole-shape – then immediately slice out to exit.

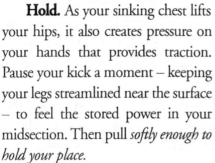

Hug. Drive your head and shoulders forward through the surface, skimming the surface with your chin. (Swim "blind" here – trying to focus your eyes will delay your head's return to

the water.) "Karate chop" your hands away from your hips, so they literally *fly* forward. Then *hug* the surface with *relaxed* arms.

Thoughts on Breathing

For a long time, coaches – convinced that breathing causes the hips to drop – urged swimmers to limit their breathing. Yet ButterStruggle leaves you breathless, because that hard-working style tenses chest muscles, making it harder to expand your lungs.

Rather than trying to "hide" your breathing errors by skipping breaths, fix them: (1) Holding the water, rather than pulling, increases breathing ease. Aid relaxation by exhaling evenly the entire time your face is in the water. (2) Hugging the surface on recovery and sinking your chest after landing keep your hips high, allowing you to breathe every stroke without hurting body position. Your muscles work better with plenty of oxygen so I recommend you breathe every stroke. The main exception is when you are learning a new drill and breathing

less frequently allows you to concentrate on the new movements.

Thoughts on Kicking

The Fly kick is often called a Dolphin Kick. Yet *dolphins don't kick*: They undulate, and so will you. Focus on *actively streamlining your legs* to extend the body wave initiated when your chest sinks and keeping your feet sub-merged. If your knees bend and feet flop out, you break your body's waveline, which increases drag and reduces power.

Keep your thighs high, as your chest sinks, and wait for your heels to reach the surface. As you land flick your toes, to help drive yourself forward into streamline.

In Speed Fly, you employ two kicks. The first – as you land – is lighter and smaller. Use it to drive your hands forward, to lengthen your body into streamline, and to tip your chest down. The second, as your hands exit, is more explosive, propulsive, and thigh-driven. This kick, synchronized with powerful movement in the core helps *catapult* the arms and upper torso forward. This is the most powerful movement in all of swimming.

You'll develop both forms of kicking far better with drills and whole stroke, than on a kickboard. Holding a board keeps your chest from sinking, removing your core muscle from the action. Consequently you kick mainly with thigh muscles when on a board – the old-style movement we're trying to unlearn. Drills and whole stroke are far better for "developing your kick" because they teach you to link leg and torso muscles in efficient whole-body movement. For the same reason I recommend you not use a pull buoy for Butterfly as that also tends to dis-integrate the upper and lower body causing you to practice ineffective movement.

BUTTERFLY: Build Your Stroke

This section will outline the steps for learning Comfort Fly and provide a sound foundation for Speed Fly.

1. Body Dolphin

Learn to extend and streamline your body and establish a sense of rhythm in your core.

- Float in balance with arms extended, and hands slightly wider than shoulders. Press and release your chest in a steady, unhurried rhythm. Each pulse should move you forward a bit.
- Keep your legs streamlined by squeezing them lightly and feel this extend the body wave to your toes. Kick by rhythmically "cracking" your knees – as you release your chest – and "flicking" your toes (i.e. lightly snapping downward) – as you press your chest.

- With each press (flick) feel your bodyline lengthen.
- Keep your head relaxed – with a "lazy chin." The angle between chin and throat should open slightly as you press (flick) and close slightly as you release (crack.) Your head should barely submerge ("Scrape the surface") as you press.

2. Include a "Sneaky Breath"

- Rehearse breathing by crouching in shallow water, bend forward until face submerges. Practice lifting head an inch or less to breathe in the small space between mouth and water. Keep your chin still – *avoid head nodding.*
- Resume Body Dolphin practice, breathing with chin in water, looking down, head steady.
- Breathe every 3 to 5 cycles initially, then gradually increase frequency until you're able to breathe smoothly each cycle.
- Rather than lifting your chin to breathe, let it occur within your undulation. When you crack your knees, your head rises naturally – breathe as your mouth clears the water.
- Keep your eyes unfocused, or even close them as you breathe. Waiting for eyes to focus will delay your head's return to the water.
- Fit breathing into the chest-pressing rhythm you established earlier.

Body Dolphin Practice Tips

Body Dolphin (BD) is most useful as a warmup or body-tuner for the other drills in this sequence and far more effective for creating "smart muscles" than kickboard sets.

1. If you don't move forward – because of stiff ankles or a tight lower back – wear full-bladed fins (we like Slim Fins best) for practice. Fins help by flexing when ankles don't, and lengthening your leg-line which helps you better respond to upper body undulation. Use fins stay to relaxed rather than to break speed records.

2. Doing BD underwater – for 3 to 5 quick cycles – will teach you to keep your undulation more compact and rhythmic.

3. You'll improve your practice with the following Focal Points, working from your hands down to your feet:

- Keep your hands *light* and moving forward with each press.
- Keep head movement subtle. Avoid head nodding. Chin at the surface as you breathe. Back of head barely below the surface as you press.
- When you focus on your legs, simply flick your toes rhythmically, keeping your feet submerged.

4. Focus more on synchronization than power while learning.

Rehearsal: Water Angels

This exercise will teach you to recover with a relaxed, surface-hugging movement.

Float with your face in the water and arms and legs extended, flutter kicking lightly as needed, or support your legs with a foam buoy. Sweep your arms back and forth in the top layer of water between a 10/2 o'clock position (forward but outside your shoulder line) – and a 4/8 o'clock position (wide of the thighs.) Arms should remain relaxed but sweep through the widest possible arc, right at the surface. Do this gently to avoid moving forward or back as your arms sweep.

3. Ride the Wave

This teaches you to slide your chest forward over anchored hands – using more core than arm muscle – then use the sweeping, relaxed recovery you learned above.

- Start with a Body Dolphin reaching wide as you press.
- Anchor your hands, slide your chest forward and "flick." This should feel like "riding a wave."
- Sweep forward as in Water Angels: (1) Arms just below the surface. (2) Lead with thumbs and reach wide. (3) Sweep hands to where you set them in Body Dolphin and flick again as you streamline.

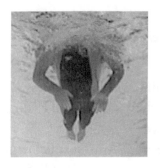

Ride the Wave Practice Tips:

1. Develop your coordination by building patiently from a single cycle to several: Pulse, slide chest forward, pulse, STOP. Repeat this until you can "slide forward" seamlessly between two pulses. When you can do this smoothly, add the sweep forward: Pulse, slide chest forward, pulse, sweep arms forward, pulse, STOP. Repeat this until you can fit the slide-forward and the sweep-forward seamlessly between pulses, without interrupting your rhythm. Continue building this way until you can complete three full cycles in a smooth rhythm. Do this without breathing.

2. Next add breathing – as in Body Dolphin – chin in water, looking down. Fit in a seamless breath as you slide forward. The breath, like the movement, should be relaxed, gentle and quiet. Minimize noise and splash.

3. Finally, focus more on using more torso muscle and less arm muscle to move forward.

4. Dolphin Dive Fly

This teaches you to land forward and enter cleanly then sink your chest to lift your legs for the next stroke.

- Dive forward, just over the surface, enter cleanly, streamline and glide until your lungs lift you to the surface. Stand and repeat. Practice until you feel yourself "riding a wave" back to the surface.

- Experiment with the depth of your dolphin dive to find the best balance between: (1) how cleanly you enter, (2) how far you travel, and (3) how easily your hips reach the surface. When you dolphin cleanly and return to the surface smoothly, continue to the next step.
- Dive forward, glide into a full stroke, re-enter, streamline and glide for distance. Stand and repeat. Practice this until: (1) your second dive/entry is as clean as the first; and (2) your streamlined glide is as fast and far as the first. Maximize relaxation, smooth movement and seamless sequencing. Add subsequent strokes one at a time, as your final stroke, entry and streamline match the feeling of the first.

Dolphin Dive Practice Tips

Your primary goal is to strive for each landing-and-streamline to feel as clean and smooth as the first. Then bring in the focus points listed below one at a time. Don't shift focus until the previous one "sinks in."

1. Each time you dive, hold your streamlined glide until your hips reach their highest point – then anchor and stroke. If you don't feel them lifting above your shoulder, dive deeper. With practice you should aim to travel forward more with your hips still lifting to the surface.

2. Each time you add another stroke, stay with that number of strokes until your final stroke, dive, and streamline feel as good as the first one in the cycle.

3. When you have progressed to four or five good strokes, begin practicing with the Focal Points listed in the training section.

Swim Comfort Fly (CF)

Once you can swim at least five good strokes of Fly, starting from a Dolphin Dive, you can begin refining your stroke.

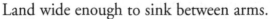

Land wide enough to sink between arms.

Keep legs *streamlined* as you hold water.

Slide head and chest *forward* over hands.

Exit hands *early*; don't push back.

Land *forward* and flick toes.

Pierce the water and let chest sink.

Using exactly the movements developed above, practice whole stroke Butterfly, taking only as many strokes as you maintain a sense of ease and relaxation. As soon as the movement feels labored or rough, STOP. As in the drill process, add whole-stroke cycles one at a time, and commit to adding only efficient movements. *Don't practice ButterStruggle for even a single cycle.*

The key to avoiding fatigue is to allow time for your chest to sink, your hands to anchor, and your hips to reach their highest point, before each stroke. If you wish to add one or two light pulses while waiting with your hands extended, do so. But I feel best when I just hold an extended bodyline and wait. This is even legal for racing. You could enter a race and do only one full stroke – and a lot of dolphins – per pool length. But you'll swim faster and more rhythmically if – rather than adding more pulses – you wait for your hips to rise fully, then stroke.

Your primary focus on the kick should be to keep your thighs near the surface at all times – and keep feet in the water. Your upper body should undulate more than your lower.

Swim Speed Fly (SF)

You swim Speed Fly with a faster, more powerful rhythm and a rhythmic 2-beat kick.

In Speed Fly, try to hold onto the water as far in front of your body as possible, but anchor more quickly. As soon as your upper chest is over your hands, release the water and whip your hands out and forward again. Swim stronger and faster by moving your torso more powerfully and quickly, not by pulling or kicking harder. When you drive your chest down more powerfully as you land, your hips and heels reach the surface more quickly, allowing you to begin your stroke more quickly.

This means you won't pause your kick to wait for your chest to sink; instead you'll maintain a steady rhythm. Though you put more energy into your kick, you should still feel as if the core-body does most of the work. The toe flick becomes a toe *snap* but still originates in your midsection.

BUTTERFLY: How to Practice

Benefits of Butterfly Practice

As I said above, practicing Fly will hone skills that benefit all your strokes and develop power in your prime-mover muscles. Plus, with a smooth Butterfly and the ability to swim lap after lap, you'll be recognized as a *complete* swimmer. As an added benefit, if you can complete 200 yards or meters of Fly at a club or Masters meet, you'll have a better chance at earning a medal than in nearly any other event because most people are so intimidated by it. Clearly, anyone who completes a 200 Fly *deserves* a medal.

The practice principle that will benefit your stroke the most is: Never practice *ButterStruggle*. The moment you can't swim or drill as described above, *stop* – even in mid-pool – and do something easier until you feel ready to drill or swim effectively. This way you'll have only efficient habits in your "muscle memory." Short repetitions are best for this purpose. I have trained champion 100-yard Flyers with few repeats longer than 20 to 25 yards, and champion 200-meter Flyers with few repeats over 50 meters.

Drill Practice

As much as in any other stroke, hone your Fly skills with drills. However, be mindful that our drill process is designed to prepare you fairly quickly to swim at least a few cycles of whole-stroke. Those few full strokes will quickly tell you whether your drill practice is leading to a relaxed, smooth style.

A key element of all drills is to maintain your core-body rhythm while fitting other movements into that rhythm. You'll begin imprinting that rhythm in Body Dolphin and should become very familiar with it as you move through the drills.

In Ride the Wave and Dolphin Dive, keep practicing just one cycle until that cycle feels good *every time*. Keep practicing just two cycles until the second cycle feels *as good as the first, every* time. This is the key strategy for building quality muscle memory. Because the potential for losing efficiency is greater than in other strokes, the fastest way to increase your Fly Endurance is by eliminating energy waste rather than increasing energy supply. And as you do condition your muscles, it will be the muscles for effective movement that become conditioned.

How to Practice Whole-Stroke

The drill process outlined above is brief and to the point, to prepare you to practice Fly via whole-stroke repeats fairly quickly. The greatest value of being capable of swimming five or six full strokes with rhythm, relaxation, and efficiency is that it allows you to practice the complete skill. While drills polish specific parts of the stroke, whole-stroke practice helps the parts work together effectively.

For instance, after perhaps five minutes of practicing Dolphin Dive with keen focus on landing your hands softly outside your shoulders, swim whole stroke for several sets of four to eight strokes. If your landing doesn't feel quite as good in whole stroke – or you lose the feeling quickly – return to Dolphin Dive practice to heighten your awareness again. If it does feel as good, you can try to deepen the imprint by maintaining that feeling with a longer series of full strokes – or move to a new drill or focal point.

Once you can swim whole stroke effectively, that doesn't mean it's time to begin "training." The usual training questions of "how many repeats, what distance, how much rest, how fast, what heart rate" are relatively unimportant as you build your capacity to swim whole stroke. The important questions are "how gentle is my landing, how patient is my catch, how relaxed is my kick" and so on.

Whole-stroke repeats are simply the skill-building stage where you integrate all the "mini-skills" you've learned through drill practice. The drills polish the parts; whole stroke practice makes those parts work well together. When you put them together, be just as strict as in drill practice about doing only as many cycles as feel efficient.

This means that many Beginning Flyers may swim only three to four strokes of full Butterfly for their first three to five hours of whole-stroke practice. Intermediate Flyers might swim nothing more than six to eight strokes for several months.

I'm now able to swim practice repeats up to 100 yards without feeling I've compromised my form, but I still swim mainly repeats of 25 yards or less, with about a third of my Fly practice as drills. Though my whole-stroke feels very good most of the time, I still gain value from drills because they allow me to give sharper attention to something fairly subtle in the stroke.

Three Types of Whole-Stroke Practice

I mentioned above that I intend to race 200 yards or meters in a Masters meet. This intention has given great clarity and purpose to my thinking about how to practice Fly. The traditional view has been that swimmers needed to train to *survive* Fly races. Coaches would assign swimmers ever-longer sets of whole-stroke Fly, on ever-briefer rest intervals, *expecting* that the swimmers' form would break down. When that happened, many coaches would drive their swimmers to push on, deep into ButterStruggle. Some coaches even gave Fly sets as punishment. No wonder many swimmers dreaded hearing the word Butterfly.

My habit as a coach has been to eradicate from muscle memory any vestige of inefficiency and replace it with smooth stroking habits, then to gradually build the swimmer's ability to maintain those strokes for greater distances or speeds. I've done this with three kinds of whole-stroke training: technique-honing with Focal Points, relaxation or "sustainability" training and speed training. I'll give examples of how I will use all three in training for my first 200 Fly race.

Focal Point Practice

I practice Focal Points mainly in 25-yard repeats, so my concentration remains sharp. Though I always keep a focal point in mind when I swim greater distances as well. I rest long enough between repeats to be able to keep my execution of that point as strong and consistent as on my first length. Those I use most frequently include:

- Landing gently – with as little noise and splash as possible

- Landing wide enough to sink my chest between my arms

- Flicking my toes as I land to give me forward momentum

- Leaving my forearms near the surface as I sink

- Waiting for my hips and/or heels to reach their highest point as I sink

- Keeping my legs streamlined – and lightly squeezed – as I sink

- Pulling softly and cracking my knees at the same moment

- Exiting my hands as soon as possible after I begin stroking

- Hugging the water with relaxed arms on recovery

- Skimming the water with my chin and looking down but "not seeing anything" as I breathe
- Exhale steadily when I'm not breathing in.

I think about one Focal Point at a time.

Sustainability Training

In conventional training this might be called Endurance Training. How far can you swim, or how many repetitions? My focus is purely to establish a sense of relaxation, and of having all parts of the stroke work effectively together. Then I test my ability to maintain that feeling for a longer swim or more short repeats, possibly with less recovery time between those reps. In Focal Point practice I might do 4 to 8 x 25 with generous rest (about 20 seconds of swimming followed by about 20 seconds of rest.) In a "Sustainability" set, I might do 12 to 16 x 25 and reduce my rest interval to 10 seconds, following 20 seconds of swimming. Or I might increase to perhaps four 50-yard repeats. Once a week I might swim a couple of 100-yard repeats. And once a month, if I have a lane to myself, I'll try a 200-yard swim. All of these Sustainability sets are just as much a test of my ability to concentrate without distraction for the entire set, as mental endurance is just as important as muscular endurance.

Speed Training

Since I intend to swim a race, I also have speed as a goal. When I swim for "speed" I change two things about my technique: (1) I flick my toes with a bit more energy to drive my body forward with a bit more momentum and speed, as I land. (2) This causes my chest to sink a bit faster, meaning I can begin my next stroke a bit sooner. What I won't do is pull harder. I focus more on feeling all the parts work together, *but just a bit faster.*

I do my speed training mainly in 25-yard repeats for a simple reason: When everything is working well together, I can swim relaxed-but-strong 25-yard repeats in 20 seconds, which equals a 200-yard pace of 2:40 (two minutes and 40 seconds). If I stretch to 50-yard repeats, the same level of effort usually brings me to the wall in 45 seconds, which equals a 200-yard pace of 3:00 (three minutes). So with 25-yard repeats and the same level of effort, I can practice at faster speed. This kind of training has helped me improve my 25-yard repeats from working fairly hard to finish in 22 seconds to being able to stay relaxed and finish in 20 seconds. My relaxed-but-strong 50-yard repeats have improved from over 50 seconds to 45 seconds in that time, so I know that my 200-yard potential has improved by quite a bit.

Whatever the distance or speed you intend to swim, training yourself to maintain relaxation and synchronization will bring you greater improvements than simply working harder or training yourself to "survive" longer.

Stroke Counting and Swim Golf

Stroke counting plays less of a role in Butterfly training than for the other strokes. Because Fly is so thoroughly a rhythm stroke, slowing your rhythm to reduce your stroke count may hurt your form. I've found that I swim nearly all my Fly lengths at just two counts in a 25-yard pool: 8 SPL when I'm emphasizing ease and flow, and 9 SPL when I try to wring a little more speed out of my CF. I may swim 8 SPL on a particularly good "speed" set of 25-yard reps, and I may swim 9 SPL, at times on a more relaxed set. And I expect I'll probably take as many as 10 SPL at some point during that first 200 Fly race. But the intentional stroke-count changing you may do in other strokes is less a part of Fly training.

Freestyle for Every Body

FREESTYLE: What You Should Know

Freestyle is most popular among swimmers because it's faster than other strokes. This leads many people to think Freestyle makes you fitter than slower strokes. It's not necessarily true – but that's another discussion. Also, the meteoric growth of triathlon has motivated thousands of runners, cyclists and others to improve their Freestyle and swim more of it.

Despite its popularity, Freestyle is the most difficult stroke to master. Alternating arm-and-leg movements are harder to learn than simultaneous arm and leg movements (as in Butterfly and Breaststroke). And breathing to the side in rhythm with alternating arm-and-leg movements is the most challenging of all swimming skills.

As with other strokes, widespread misconceptions about technique have increased the challenges described above. The traditional understanding of Freestyle technique is: Pull your arms, kick your legs, grab a breath when you can. Virtually everyone finds it difficult and uncomfortable but believe that if you grind out enough training miles, you'll develop the ability to survive a bit longer.

TI Freestyle is based on radically different concepts: balance, streamlining, a patient catch, and swimming *with* your body weight. Few humans actually swim that way – mainly high-skilled swimmers and those who have learned from TI. Why so few? (1)

Those who can swim more than a few strokes or laps are too busy grinding out miles and (2) The instinct to pull-and-kick is far more powerful than the instinct to balance-streamline-and-hold. Our goal here is to change that.

How to Minimize Drag

Raise your lower body.

Gravity pulls down your legs, while buoyancy pushes up your chest. Sinking legs create far more drag than legs that remain horizontal. Most people try to raise sinking legs by kicking harder. Leg churning not only doesn't correct your balance, it also wears you out, and interferes with rhythm and rotation. Instead, treat your body like a teeter-totter: (1) Look straight down: Aligning your head with your spine and hips helps counterbalance your legs. (2) Keep one arm forward of (and below) your head at all times, by allowing the entering hand to take over the "leading position" before the stroking hand passes your nose. This will also help you minimize drag through a more horizontal position…without the energy cost of kicking.

Pierce the Water.

Because you must swim *through* water that's 880 times denser than air, aim to cut through the water like a laser rather than power through it. Instead of "arms that pull" and "legs that kick," alternate *a right-side-streamlined position* with *a left-side-streamlined position*, keeping each side as long and sleek as possible from fingers to toes.

Visualize parallel Tracks extending forward of each shoulder and spear your arm and body down that Track. Those imaginary *Tracks* will provide direction and a positioning guide for every part of your stroke.

Lengthen your "Vessel."

The most resistant form of drag is "wave drag," the energy you spend making waves as you move through the water. Wave drag increases exponentially as you swim faster – and waves get bigger as you turn over faster. The best way to reduce wave drag – and increase speed potential – is to lengthen your bodyline. Thus a critical shift in your awareness is to replace your instinct to push water back, with a habit of using your hand to extend your bodyline. Also, slice your hand into the water sooner. Entering your hand and arm early starts the body-lengthening process sooner, and entering it cleanly *parts the water* for your much blunter head and shoulders, as they follow down the Track.

How to Create Propulsion

Hold onto your place in the water.

Extending your arm below your head will aid your balance. And entering closer to your head will improve your streamline. Here's another tip: If the fingers of your extended hand are tipped up, your legs will sag down. If your fingers are tipped down, it's far more likely your legs will be up.

Every elite Freestyler spears to a fingers-down position immediately upon entering the water – for a good reason: The fingers-down, palm-back position is best for gripping the water. Slice your arm in, as if through a mail slot, to avoid disturbing the water; quiet water allows a firmer grip. Second, reach forward until your shoulder touches your jaw. Third, "wrap your hand around the front of its Track" to trap water behind it. Fourth, anchor it there as you spear the other hand.

Creating an overlap between your arms means a faster transition from a *right-side-streamlined* to a *left-side-streamlined* position. You may be thinking all this patience will cost you speed. But if you line up like a laser on your Tracks, you'll maintain enough speed to give yourself time to do each of these with care. And the firmer your grip, the faster you'll travel as you spear past it.

Swim *with* your body weight.

In traditional Freestyle you muscle your body through the water by pulling and kicking. In TI Freestyle, you align your body to slip through the water, then use weight shift to create more efficient propulsion. While your right side is streamlined on its Track, your left side will be rolled above the surface. As your left arm comes forward, gravity triggers a weight shift onto that side. Spearing forward helps accelerate that shift to produce effortlessly powerful movement. To do that, focus on *spearing your hand through an imaginary target* at the front of your Track. You'll locate that target during the Skating drill. The energy released by spearing will *vault you past your gripping hand,* which is anchored on the Right Track. Arms that *push* water tire quickly. Arms that *hold* the water can be nearly tireless.

Breathe Two Ways

Alternate-side or bilateral breathing promotes symmetry better than single side breathing. If you breathe only to one side, it's likely that you'll veer off the Tracks in that direction. I try to breathe as often to each side in practice, and when racing. Breathing to your unfamiliar side may feel awkward at first, but patient practice will gradually reduce that awkwardness. As well, all the drills described in the next section improve symmetry and build a better foundation for efficient bilateral breathing. I'll expand on breathing mechanics in the next section.

Kick Two Ways

Accomplished Freestylers tend to favor one of two flutter-kicking styles. Sprinters favor a *6-beat kick* in which there are six beats to every full arm cycle (i.e. from right hand entry to right hand entry). Distance swimmers, as well as fitness swimmers and triathletes, generally do better with a *2-beat kick*. In the 2-beat, the right foot downbeat should synchronize with the left-hand entry and vice versa. The 2-beat uses less energy and synchronizes well with the spearing emphasis we'll teach here, so we'll devote more attention to that style. I'll expand on kicking mechanics in the next section.

FREESTYLE: Build Your Stroke

Because Freestyle skills are more complex than those for other strokes, allow as much time as necessary to become comfortable with each skill-building step.

Get the air you need.

Unless you have all the air you need, you'll be too distracted to concentrate on other skills during drill practice. Being mindful of the following will be helpful as you rotate from nose-up to nose-down and back again:

Don't hold your breath. Begin exhaling immediately. Exhaling with slow quiet *nose* bubbles is a good way to regulate your breathing *and* to avoid inhaling water or choking as you breathe.

Blow the water away. Exhale with more force as your face clears the surface – as if trying to blow the water away from your nose and mouth.

Relax into the water. If you lift your head, it will be harder to get air. If you keep your head low, it will be easier. And stay relaxed whenever you are rolling up to get air, or back down. Moving abruptly in either direction will make your body position less stable.

Step One: Balance Sequence

Rehearse Skating Position: Lie in Skating position on the floor – balanced on one side with lower arm extended, directly forward of your shoulder, palm down. Splay your feet slightly to help stabilize you. Imprint the following: (1) Nose to floor. (2) Touch jaw to shoulder. (3) Extend arm on "Track," not in center. (4) Other hand in "Jeans Pocket."

Skating

Teaches: (1) the essential "side-streamlined" position for Freestyle; (2) front-to-back balance and side-to-side stability; (3) awareness of the Tracks you'll follow through the water.

- Streamline on one side, looking down, and extending that arm below your head and on its Track, with shoulder touching your jaw. Relax your extended hand until fingers point down.
- Rest the other hand on your front thigh and reach it toward your knee.
- Flutter kick gently and concentrate on streamlining your legs.
- Switch to the other Track on the next length.

To Breathe:

- Roll back until you're nearly on your back. *Keep arm extended; turn palm up.*
- Move head and body as one and *relax back* as you roll up.
- Breathe easily until you feel relaxed and comfortable before returning to Skating position.

Skating Practice Tips

- Experiment with the depth of the extended arm and hand, until your legs feel "light." If your hand is relaxed enough to hang limply, your arm angle can be less steep.
- Also experiment with the degree of rotation that allows you to feel most stable on the Track. Too much on your stomach will move your hand outside the Track. "Stacked shoulders" will move it toward the other Track.

- Memorize your hand location – both depth and track position. This will become the "target" to which you'll spear your hand in all Switch drills – and in whole stroke.
- Focus on rotating as a unit and maintain laserlike alignment as you rotate up to breathe and back down to streamline on the Track.

Advanced Breathing Skill: "Bite of Air"

If you began this sequence already breathing comfortably in Freestyle, you can try an advanced breathing skill. Rather than rolling to Sweet Spot for air, try to breathe with minimal shoulder rotation and with goggles and mouth right at the surface, while keeping the extended hand angled down. Whichever breathing style you choose, keep it leisurely and relaxed.

Step Two: UnderSwitch Sequence

Teaches you: (1) To streamline each side of your body on the Track; (2) To move forward by spearing forward; and (3) To keep a patient lead hand as you spear.

- Start in Skating position on your Right Track. "Sneak" your left hand up the track from your thigh to your goggles – keep elbow tight to your ribs and turn palm up.

- Pause hand at goggles to check that you're still on the Right Track with left shoulder above the surface.

- Spear your left hand to the "target" established in Skating. Pause to check that you're in the same position imprinted in Skating, then repeat in the other direction.

- Do one or two more Switches this way, then roll to Sweet Spot and get all the air you need before returning to Skating to begin switching again.

UnderSwitch Practice Tips

1.   Initially, you may do only one or two switches before rotating to Sweet Spot for air, because of pausing for a moment to examine your Track position before and after the Switch. Devote several minutes or lengths to each of these Focal Points before adding additional switches:

- After pausing hand at goggles, Switch both hands at the same moment.
- Spear hand to "target" and align your body – also spearlike – on the Track.

- Visualize the hood of a VW Beetle in front of you. From goggles, slide your hand across hood and *down to the bumper* – i.e. reaching fingers down as you reach full extension.

- Trap water behind a stationary hand (i.e. it stands still for a moment) before switch.

2.   When those Focal Points begin to feel natural, increase the number of switches by gradually eliminating the pauses between switches and by:

- Rotate only enough to clear your shoulder and hip from the water on each switch.
- Keep your stroking hand moving. Finish stroke and *immediately* begin recovery as a seamless uninterrupted movement.

3.   If you were comfortable with the "bite of air" breathing technique in Skating, you may experiment with breathing that way in USwitches, rather than pausing in Sweet Spot. But be mindful that *getting all the air you need* is essential to skilled practice.

Step Three: ZipperSwitch Sequence

These two drills – ZipperSkate and ZipperSwitch – teach a compact, relaxed recovery and help connect hip-drive to your spearing arm.

ZipperSkate Rehearsal.

Practice the Zipper recovery on the floor, in the same position in which you rehearsed Skating.

- Lie on your Left
  Track with left hand
  aligned with shoul-
  der, nose to floor,
  and jaw touching
  shoulder. Right hand

  in your "jeans pocket" reaching toward knee.
- Starting with a small outward movement of your right
  elbow, draw your arm forward. Lead with elbow and hand
  trailing slightly behind, fingertips lightly brushing the floor.
  Keep forearm and elbow an inch or two from your torso.
- When elbow reaches your ear, feel your arm hanging loosely from your elbow "like a marionette."
- Repeat several times with a focus on elbow leading hand for
  as long as possible. Repeat on other side.

ZipperSkate

*Teaches how to use the weight of an arm suspended alongside your
ear as a "tipping point" for better balance.*

- While kicking gently in
  Skating position, draw
  your arm forward as in
  floor rehearsal.

- Pause when hand "catches
  up" to elbow. Feel "tipping
  forward" sensation caused
  by the weight of your arm suspended just forward of your
  lungs.
- Return arm to starting point, roll up to Sweet Spot and
  breathe before repeating. Practice on both sides.

ZipperSkate Practice Tips

- Begin each recovery by *circling elbow slightly outside*, rather than lifting it behind you.
- Keep each arm "on the Tracks." Both arms should be equidistant from centerline for side-to-side stability. Check this while pausing with arm suspended by ear.
- Bring arm forward as slowly as possible. Lead with your elbow and soften your arm so hand lags behind.
- If you have enough breath, you may repeat the Zipper recovery two or three times before rotating to Sweet Spot.

ZipperSwitch

Connects hip drive to spearing/propelling action and reinforces Patient Catch.

- While Skating on your Right Track, draw left hand slowly forward as above.

- Pause hand at ear. It should be directly below elbow.

- Feel your right hand – fingers down – trapping water gently, then spear suspended hand from your ear to its "target".

- Pause a moment to check Left Track position before drawing right hand forward to repeat.

ZipperSwitch Practice Tips

1.   Initially you may do only one or two switches before rotating to Sweet Spot for air, because of pausing to check Track position before and after the Switch. Practice these Focal Points until each feels natural:

- Feel the powerful-but-effortless propulsion that results from spearing from ear to "target".
- Focus on feeling that your high-side hip and your opposite foot both drive your hand to the target.
- Maintain a firm grip as you switch.
- Keep both arms on their Tracks.

2. When those Focal Points begin to feel natural, increase the number of switches by gradually eliminating the pause alongside your ear and by:

- Rotate only enough to clear your shoulder and hip from the water on each switch.
- Keep your stroking hand moving to begin recovery as a seamless uninterrupted movement.
- Feel yourself gliding effortlessly along the Track as you draw your hand forward.

3. If you were comfortable with the "bite of air" breathing technique in UnderSwitch, you may experiment with that breathing technique, rather than pausing in Sweet Spot.

Step Four: Transition to Whole Stroke

Teaches a compact, relaxed recovery, reinforces Patient Catch and imprints a deft, clean entry and solid grip to connect hip drive to spearing arm. Also integrates breathing into the stroke rhythm.

- For your first several repeats, begin each length with several ZipperSwitches, then lift hand so it barely clears the surface and dips back into the water almost immediately.
- Do two or more such switches, then rotate to Sweet Spot for a breath – or breathe normally if you're comfortable doing so.
- Focus on recovery and entry first, by using the following Focal Points, one at a time:

1. Ear Hops. Visualize a bar extending from each ear. Hop fingers over this imaginary bar and immediately return to water. Hand should clear water as briefly as possible.

2. Marionette Arms. Feel as if elbow is suspended from a string and forearm and hand hang from the elbow like a marionette – completely relaxed.

3. Mail Slot Imagine a "mail slot" on the Tracks. Slipping your hand into the Slot will be easy. Sliding your forearm through will take care.

Next focus on establishing a Patient Catch, using these Focal Points:

1. Fingers down....Keep fingers tipped down throughout extension, feeling light water pressure on your palm as you reach downward.

2. Make hand stand still for a brief moment before stroking.

3. Begin the stroke, just as – or just before your other hand enters the Mail Slot.

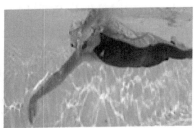

Rhythmic Breathing

Three tips for fitting a seamless rhythmic breath into your stroke, while maintaining good balance and a Patient Catch.

Follow your shoulder. As you spear one arm forward, the opposite shoulder moves back. Just follow this shoulder with your chin and the rotational energy of spearing will make it easier to get air.

Stay low. Practice this in three ways: (1) *Relax into the water* as you breathe; (2) Keep the top of your head as close to the surface as possible, while rolling to breathe; (3) Look back slightly over your shoulder as you breathe.

Stay "tall." Give extra care to keeping the lead hand "patient" as you breathe, stroking only after you inhale. And if you keep your fingers tipped down, your next stroke will be far stronger.

Improve Your Kick

Tips for improving a non-propulsive kick and "tuning" your kick to work in harmony with the rest of your body.

Why do I go backward?

I expect that many readers of this book will be improvement-minded adults who have recently begun swimming seriously for the first time. Many such adults have had the experience of standing still – or even going backward – while using a kickboard. Inflexible ankles are a common cause. We all lose flexibility as we age (unless you follow a dedicated stretching or yoga program) and if you didn't start swimming young, you may then spend 20 to 40 years gradually losing ankle flexibility. Years of running accelerates the stiffening process. If you started swimming young, and continued, you have probably maintained better ankle flexibility.

Another common cause is lack of coordination. Most of your other kicking experiences (soccer balls, tires, your little brother) teach you to kick with about 90 degrees of knee flexion – which uses mainly quadriceps (thigh) muscle. An efficient flutter kick flexes less than 30 degrees; the kick happens mostly from the hip flexor and abdominals. Kids do it naturally; the adult-onset swimmer often has to unlearn improper kicking habits in order to learn the right way. The following are effective ways to develop a more efficient kick:

Seated kicking. Sit on the edge of the pool with most of your legs dangling in the water and move the water back and forth with a nearly-straight leg. Try "stirring" the water with one foot to develop a bit more awareness of how to feel the water with your feet.

Vertical kicking. Do this in deeper water, while hugging a kickboard to your chest. Focus on keeping a long line from hip to toes as you kick. Your leg should be long and supple, never rigid. To avoid over-flexing your knees, lead with your heel as you kick back, and with the top of your foot as you kick forward.

Side kicking. The Sweet Spot and Skating drills are ideal for transferring the action you develop in Vertical Kick (VK) to a horizontal position. Use VK to imprint the pattern, then maintain while drilling.

Using fins. The primary benefit of fins is that the blade flexes, compensating for the ankle that won't. Using fins during drill practice also allows you to relax so you can pay attention to more subtle sensations. If loss of momentum during the Sweet Spot pause is distracting and tiring, consider using fins during drill practice, but we recommend removing them to swim.

Integrate kick while swimming. Unless your goal is to race 100 meters at top speed, we advocate a non-overt kick – i.e. one you're hardly aware of. Balance practice helps eliminate the "nervous legs" syndrome, making it easier to coordinate your legs with your arms and hips. For a 2-beat kick, try to coordinate a single leg beat to each arm stroke. As your right hand spears, drive your left foot down, and vice versa. This may be easier to learn in ZipperSwitch. Pause your feet when you pause your hand at your ear, then drive the opposite foot as you spear to the "target." Do this with a light kick at first, then drive the foot more powerfully until you can feel it add to the energy of your arm-spear.

FREESTYLE: How To Practice

Because most readers are likely to swim Freestyle more often than other strokes, I'll provide more detail here on how to practice it, but virtually all suggestions I make for Freestyle apply as well to the other three strokes.

Phase One: Develop Comfort, Control and Self-Awareness

Every swimmer who is new to TI Practice should devote a minimum of 10 to 20 hours of practice to the activities suggested for this phase – though some swimmers have remained at this level for a year or two without stagnating or becoming bored.

Your goals in Phase One are to make relaxation and ease routine, to improve your awareness of how your body behaves in the water, to minimize the UHSP (see Chapter Two), and develop basic habits of efficient, fluent movement. Drills are more effective than whole-stroke for accomplishing these goals. When your comfort and self-awareness in whole-stroke begin to match your drills, you can include more swimming. The specific foundations you should be forming in this phase include:

- Make breathing routine so it's not a distraction while working on the next three foundations;
- Find effortless support or balance, by imprinting a neutral head position and the right position on the Track for your (relaxed) extended hand;
- Make long, "slippery" bodylines a habit by learning to "pierce the water" with your spearing arm and follow the Track with your bodyline;
- Make whole-body propelling movements a habit.

Tools:

- **30% Balance Drills** (Sweet Spot, Skating and ZipperSkate) to find your balance and imprint sleek bodylines.

- **40% Under- and ZipperSwitch Drills.** Focus on minimizing drag and turbulence and becoming "patient" in trapping the water.
- **20% Mindful Swimming** (whole stroke with focal points) to transfer the awareness gained in drills into whole stroke.
- **10% Stroke Counting** to measure your improvements in efficiency and compare the effectiveness of various focal points.

Phase One Practice Tips

Until you overcome the UHSP tendencies that have limited your efficiency, almost any whole-stroke swimming is likely to reinforce those habits and delay improvement. The fastest way to break "struggling habits" is to replace whole-stroke laps with *whatever allows you to practice fluent movement.* For most new TI Swimmers, that means drills.

Making efficient, fluent swimming a habit starts with exploring basic movements and positions with a sense of curiosity – and no sense of urgency. Any time you feel even minor discomfort during a drill, your natural reaction will be some kind of compensation – craning your neck, sculling, kicking too hard. These unconscious reactions imprint energy-wasting movements on your nervous system. Thus avoiding them is essential.

Patience in mastering basic skills may be natural to martial artists and dancers, but not to most swimmers. I only came to appreciate its value after beginning regular yoga practice. So here is a goal for your first 10 to 20 hours of TI Practice: Simply learn to make mindful, examined movement a habit. Don't count laps or watch the pace clock; focus purely on reducing effort and increasing flow.

Your period of concentrated drill practice may last a few weeks to several months. The drills described herein will be your primary vehicle for changing habits and it's best to commit

them to muscle-memory, while reading this book. Your drill
practice will benefit greatly if you follow these guidelines:

- **Short repeats.** 25 yards/meters or less for the first several
  weeks, and seldom longer than 50 yards/meters.
- **Short sets.** To maintain close attention, change your focus
  every 10 minutes or so. Alternate tasks that require intense
  focus, with those that require less concentration.
- **Clear focus.** Think about doing *just one thing well* on each
  length. E.G. on ZipperSwitches you could divide your Focal
  Points into head position, keeping your arm "deep and
  slow" during recovery, leading with your elbow, slicing your
  hand from ear to target, tipping your fingertips down, being
  patient with your catch.
- **Ignore the clock.** Use deep, relaxing breaths (known in med-
  itation and yoga as "cleansing breaths") to regulate your rest
  interval between repeats. 3 to 5 breaths should be sufficient.
- **Swim moderately.** Swimming whole stroke for 10 to 20 percent of total practice time is a good way to explore the
  changes your new awareness is creating. Mainly focus on sensations created during the drills and how they transfer to
  whole-stroke.

Phase Two: Develop Your Stroke

This phase will typically take between several months (for
those who adapt quickly to new skills) and several years (for
those who have the deepest habits of struggle to unlearn or are
least comfortable initially). Your goals in this phase are to build
upon the comfort, body awareness and coordinated-movement
habits developed in the Foundation Phase by learning to swim
the whole stroke with the same degree of balance, ease and control that you enjoyed in the drills. You do that by:

- Learning to swim "balanced and tall."
- Learning to fit a rhythmic breath into your stroke without

interrupting your flow and while keeping a hand extended and anchored.

- Learning to start each stroke with a "patient hand" – i.e. having the time and presence of mind to cultivate a firm grip on the water before stroking.

- Establish an SPL (strokes per length) range of three to four 25-yd/mtr stroke counts (e.g. 15 to 18 SPL) at which you can swim efficiently...and (2) be able to swim 400 to 1500 meters without exceeding your SPL range...and (3) to swim sets of shorter repeats (repeats of 25 to 200 yds or meters in sets that last 10 to 20 minutes) in the lower half of your SPL range.

Tools:

- **10% Balance Drills** (more ZipperSkate, less Sweet Spot) mainly for warmup or recovery.

- **40% Switch Drills** Focus mainly on Pierce-and-Track, and on using your lead hand to "hold onto your place" in the water, while spearing your other hand forward.

- **20% Mindful Swimming** both in drill/swim sets and in pure swimming sets

- **20% Stroke Counting and Gears** practice to increase your ability to choose your SPL at will and to add strokes as a means of gaining speed.

- **10% Swim Golf** to begin measuring the effect of various stroke counts and focal points. Find description of Gears and Swim Golf in the chapter on Training.

Phase Two Practice Tips

Following a period of intensive drill practice, you have two priorities: (1) Apply what you've learned in drills to whole-stroke swimming and (2) Begin imprinting an economical stroke into your muscle memory.

It takes between 7000 (for simple skills) and 20,000 (for more complex skills) CORRECT repetitions to move a new skill from conscious control to auto-pilot. That could translate into about 100,000 yards of thinking about "hanging your head" or "tipping your fingers down" to make each a permanent part of your stroke.

The two key ingredients to Stroke Development training are Drill-Swim Sets and Mindful Swimming:

Drill/Swim. Drill practice not only teaches new skills; it also makes you more aware of sensations that signal how you're positioned – i.e. is your head aligned, are you on the Tracks – or the timing of important movements. In part, they simply make you feel *good* in the water. In Drill-Swim sets, your primary objective is to focus on whatever feels good in the drill and make it feel the same while doing whole stroke. At first, it might take you 75 yards of a drill to feel the sensation clearly, and you might be able to maintain that feeling for only 25 yards of swimming. Later that mix will become 50 yards drill and 50 swim, then 25 drill and 75 swim. Always be clear on what you're trying to feel. If you're focused on head position while drilling, stay with that focus on your swim laps.

Mindful Swimming. When you feel ready to try some sets that are exclusively or mainly whole-stroke swimming, this is the first practice form to use, because it simplifies and concentrates your task. In this form of swimming, you give all your attention to Focal Points, which you began doing in Drill/Swim sets. Count strokes only if you can maintain focus on the feeling you've chosen. Stroke counting can be a good way to compare the effectiveness of one Focal Point with another. How does your SPL compare when you focus on *spearing* vs. when you focus on the *mail slot*? Here are some sample Focus Points for Freestyle:

- Hang your Head – i.e. release its weight to the water.
- Slip your arm through a *mail slot* on entry.

- Make your hands *stand still* for a moment before stroking.
- Spear forward – "finish" each stroke to the front, not back.
- Chin follows shoulder as you breathe.

Each of these focal points works on a different part of the stroke. And each lap you consciously focus on, say, slipping your arm into a mail slot faintly imprints a new groove in your nervous system. After five or 10 minutes thinking only about that, it will feel a bit more natural and improve the chances that you'll continue doing it when you're thinking about something else.

One training idea might be to write down your favorite Focal Points on an index card, put that card in a waterproof cover, and take it to the pool with you. Leave it at the end of your lane, and then do 4 X 25 of each Focal Point on the card. Allow enough time between 25s to catch your breath and think about how you feel. As they become easier, progress to 4 X 50 of each cue. Then 4 X 75. The level of focus required to do these and groove them into your nervous system makes the time fly, so enjoy this exercise in Mindful Swimming, while you build efficiency and fitness.

Phase Three: Increase Mastery, Distance and Speed

Your goals in this phase are to be able to increase your awareness, control and coordination to swim farther and faster with the least additional effort. Your specific training goals are:
- Develop the ability to choose any SPL and swim effectively.
- Develop the ability to increase your speed without increasing your SPL, while maintaining a sense of relaxation.
- Swim near your "red line" with control and gradually raise your red line.
- Be able to apply everything you do in practice while racing.

Tools:

- **20% Drills** – focused on stroke timing, patient catch, and trapping water
- **30% Mindful Swimming** – in drill-swim sets and whole-stroke sets
- **20% Stroke Counting and Gears**
- **20% Swim Golf or Descending Series**
- **10% Distance Development**

Phase Three Practice Tips

In Phase One, your main goal was to develop an "aquatic brain." Your "land brain" is expert at managing balance and movement when you are stable, subject to gravity and vertical. Your "aquatic brain" must learn to manage your body when you are unstable, subject to resistance and horizontal. During Phase Two you applied your aquatic brain to memorizing the movements of an efficient Freestyle.

In Phase Three – which continues for the rest of your life – you have three goals: (1) Continue developing and refining your skills, particularly a firm, stable catch and breathing so you get all the air you need without compromising your form. I call these "evolving" skills because you can continue refining them, and deepening your awareness, for decades. After 40 years of swimming and nearly 20 years of TI practice I still make noticeable gains in these skills each year. (2) Learn to swim farther without fatigue or loss of efficiency. (3) Learn to swim faster while minimizing fatigue and loss of efficiency. In pursuit of this final goal, we will begin to use the pace clock (or sports watch) as a measuring tool, in Swim Golf or Descending Sets. But as you can see from the percentages assigned above for each training tool, timed sets are still a relatively minor part of the whole program.

Your Drill Practice will focus more on Switch drills, and particularly ZipperSwitch, as that's closest to whole stroke, and drill-only sets will become less frequent than drill/swim sets. Your Mindful Swimming focal points will focus on 'problem solving' and you might choose to focus on one "problem" for a period of some months. My main focus for the last six months has been to catch water more firmly with my right hand, while taking a left-side breath. Prior to that, it was to hold the water a bit longer with my lead hand, while spearing.

In Stroke Counting, you will focus a bit less on holding a certain count for longer distances – or on reducing the lowest count in your SPL range – and a bit more on being able to change counts at will without losing efficiency as well to feel your speed increase when you add a stroke or two to your SPL.

In Swim Golf and Descending sets, you'll make the pace clock a primary tool for evaluating your swimming. Can you swim faster without increasing your SPL? Or can you gain a bit more speed when increasing your SPL by one stroke, than you had previously. The one constant will be to maximize your speed while minimizing your effort or controlling your stroke count.

In Distance Development, you seek to increase the distance you can swim *efficiently* without straining and without stopping. If your SPL range is 14 to 17 strokes, how far can you swim with an SPL of 14. Perhaps it's only 50 yards initially? With practice can you extend that to 200 yards – or to a set of 10 x 50 on 10 seconds rest? And if you can swim 200 yards while maintaining an SPL of 15, can you extend that to 500 yards, or to a set of 8 x 100 on 15 seconds rest. At any stroke count simply make it a goal to increase the distance you can complete nonstop *without strain* at a given stroke count. You can also increase that distance by doing a recovery length of your favorite drill or a different stroke when your SPL climbs above your target count, then resume swimming at the target SPL. I'll include more detail and suggestions on these forms of practice in the TI Training chapter that follows.

Total Immersion Training

Effective Training vs. Traditional Training

This section is not intended be the last word on training. That would take an entire book (to be will published in 2007.) But the information here will help you begin planning your own practices – or help you get more benefit from practices you may be doing with a coached group or team. By understanding how to train for Continuous Improvement, you'll use your pool time more effectively, enjoy the experience more fully, and reach your goals more consistently.

Several years ago, I copied these sentences from an article describing a training session by a world champion track athlete: "For nearly three hours, she skims over 10 hurdles set 10 meters apart, tirelessly solving tiny biomechanical problems that keep her from running fractionally faster than anyone else. On each repeat, she focuses on keeping her feet below her center of mass, which helps her explode efficiently over each hurdle, reducing learned muscular actions to nearly automatic responses."

Such meticulous focus on an exacting skill is radically different from the grind-it-out conditioning sessions that most people think of as "training." While running hurdles is a demanding skill, so is moving efficiently in a medium as uncooperative as water. Thus, while traditional training focuses on building your aerobic system, Effective Training focuses first on your nervous system, on developing movement efficiency. I.E., we give as much attention to reducing energy cost as to increasing energy stores.

Traditional workouts often seem intended to make you tired. Technique is usually an afterthought – something to do when you need a breather. That approach may improve endurance, but it also tends to deepen your "struggling skills," meaning you burn through that endurance more quickly. And it often leads to injury. Finally, it wastes precious time: It takes at least twice as long to unlearn a bad habit, and replace it with a good one, as to learn it right the first time.

This section will help you create a program designed to *train your strokes* – first to do them efficiently, then to transform new movements into enduring habits and finally to strengthen your ability to remain efficient as you swim faster. Your increased efficiency will lead to greater endurance, not just by increasing your fitness, but by allowing you to go farther on the energy you already have. And being able to go farther will help you develop your fitness even more. The first step is to set goals for your training.

Goals That Transform

Like the goal of Continuous Improvement which I described in Chapter Two, your most transforming goals will be more expansive than "Swim 100 meters in under 1:20" or "Swim a mile nonstop." Since age 50, I've been mindful of two goals every time I swim. These have been instrumental in helping me improve substantially at an age when most swimmers are slowing down. If they make sense to you, I encourage you to make them your own.

Goal #1: Every time I enter the water, I aim to swim *better than I ever have in my life*. Setting the goal that high keeps me intently focused. Before making this a conscious objective, I had many practices that felt somewhat routine. No more. Now, I finish virtually every practice with a sense that I've done something truly worthwhile – and often exhilarating. A key to making such a lofty goal achievable is that my "best-evers" are many and varied, ranging from swimming a series of 100-yard Freestyle repeats on 12SPL with more ease than before, to better integration of a short, quick kick in Breaststroke, a smoother left-hand entry in Backstroke, to the day I swam a surprisingly relaxed 200 Fly for the first time. What I love about this goal is that it creates a sense of exciting possibility every time I enter the water.

Goal #2: On every set, my goal is to accomplish any task I set myself (whether technique, stroke count, time or some combination) with as little effort as possible. In conventional training, as I mentioned above, the goal is typically to work *harder*. But time and energy are finite, while opportunities to increase efficiency and relaxation are virtually limitless. After 40 years of swim training, I'm still improving my ability to swim with great economy, and at age 55 I'm racing better than ever because I'm steadily increasing my ability to stay relaxed while swimming near my top speed. All because greater ease, rather than greater effort, is my goal at the beginning of every set.

Take Effective Action.

The surest way to transform goals into reality is by rigorously devoting every minute and movement toward specific outcomes, rather than being satisfied to simply add to your yardage total. Because efficient swimming requires you to solve a challenging puzzle – how to move effectively in an uncooperative and unnatural medium – you can't afford to waste a minute on ineffective action (e.g. kickboard sets, unfocused repeat series, mind*less* rather than mindful swimming, or *any* inefficient movement). On every lap, link your actions to one of the dozens of skill goals outlined throughout this book.

What about Endurance?

The dictionary defines *endurance* as "the ability to resist fatigue or withstand a prolonged stressful effort." Total Immersion defines *swimming endurance* as "the ability to repeat *effective swimming movements* for a duration and speed of your choosing." This definition places as much emphasis on nervous system (muscle memory) development as on aerobic system development. But there's a critical difference: When you make nervous system training your first priority, the aerobic system always gets trained too. When you make aerobic system training your first priority, there's no guarantee the nervous system will be trained effectively – and it is often sacrificed to "pushing through pain barriers." To be sure, TI Training doesn't ignore conditioning. Rather, we define conditioning as "something that happens" as you practice effective movement" – an approach exemplified by that world champion hurdler.

Swimming for Fitness

Many of those who read this book swim purely for fitness, and may wonder: "If I'm swimming more efficiently, won't I lose fitness?" Here are four reasons why it pays to be efficient for lifelong calorie burning, injury-free swimming and enjoyment:
1. You burn calories most effectively by using large muscle groups which have been trained for endurance, especially the "core" muscles in your abdominals and back. "Human" swimming, with its focus on pulling and kicking, relies heavily on arm and leg muscles that fatigue before the real calorie burning begins. Every drill and skill in this book is designed to promote

better integration of your arms and legs with core muscles that are highly fatigue resistant and provide a better workout.

2. TI Practice focuses on balance, alignment, and coordinated, fluent movement. Sound biomechanics make good use of the body, minimize the chances of injury and increase the likelihood that you'll be able to continue healthful training consistently. The best outcome for your health and fitness is to swim pain-free each day and avoid overuse fatigue.

3. Motivation matters. If your fitness routine is enjoyable and stimulating, you're more likely to continue for the long term. The prospect of Continued Improvement will keep you swimming far more than doing it just because "it's good for you."

4. Finally, it's always an option to increase your intensity. Once you master the basics and increase your efficiency, longer and faster swims, with less fatigue, will become the norm.

Should I Increase Yardage?

A key principle of TI Training is that the primary reason for swimming more yards is *to increase your opportunities to imprint efficient movement.* You can make such a choice either to accelerate your learning process on a particular skill or deepen your muscle memory and make it more immune to breakdown as you swim farther or faster. Will fitness also increase as you do so? Yes it will, but your swimming will benefit most if skill improves along with fitness. So if increased yardage causes you to compromise the quality of your strokes, perhaps you shouldn't do it. A mantra to guide you in all such questions is" "Never Practice Struggle."

The critical characteristic of Effective Training is that learning should occur in virtually every practice. So our next chapter will examine how skill development happens and how you can learn more and faster.

EFFECTIVE TRAINING

How to Keep Your Learning on the Fast Track

There are four stages in the mastery of any skill. In the first stage, *Unconscious Incompetence*, we perform ineffectively, but don't understand why. When we grasp what needs fixing and why, we achieve the state of *Conscious Incompetence*. In learning a new drill or skill, it takes constant attention to get it right. That's *Conscious Competence*. The drawback here is that it's difficult to swim fast or fluently when you're thinking instead of feeling.

Fortunately, as you continue to practice, you sense that something has become so ingrained – e.g. keeping your head aligned and legs streamlined as you spread your hands in Butterfly or Breaststroke – that you can give your full attention to another important detail, i.e. *holding* water as you begin the stroke. That's *Unconscious Competence* – at least for that particular piece of coordination. And that's a critical realization in training your strokes: As soon as you achieve the goal of Unconscious Competence in one skill, you should immediately return to Conscious Competence in another.

The second critical phenomenon that can ease your progress is called "chunking." It's been estimated that it can take 10 or more years to reach the grandmaster level in chess. The difference between grandmasters and players who are merely good, is that great players are adept at "chunking" dozens, and sometimes hundreds, of possible moves into a consolidated information set which frees them from having to consider each move separately.

We work with short-term memory at the Conscious Competence level, then shift to long-term memory as we progress to Unconscious Competence. Because short-term memory can only handle a few bits of information at once, chunking becomes essential to coordinating more complex skills. A good example of chunking is how you probably learned to read: Step 1: Sound out each word, one syllable at a time. Step 2: Digest a full line of text by picking out a few key words but your speed is still limited by needing to move your eyes horizontally across the line and vertically to a new line. Step 3: Take in full paragraphs by using contextual clues to pick out key phrases. This is how Speed Readers can race down an entire page in just seconds.

For a swimming example of chunking at work, let's consider how you'll start developing your Freestyle with the Skating position, which is essential to efficiency in the whole stroke. When you first practice Skating, you might spend time examining up to 10 separate pieces of information:

- Am I bubbling quietly from my nose?
- Am I relaxing my neck and "hanging" my head?
- Are my head and spine aligned?
- Is my extended hand on its Track?
- Is that hand "hanging" so my fingers point down?
- Is my other hand "in the pocket" on my front thigh?
- Are both arms equidistant from my spine?
- Am I flutter kicking within my bodyline?
- Am I rotated so one shoulder clears the water?
- Is my bodyline "toned" but not tense?

After 10 or more hours on many self-checks, your awareness will gradually consolidate into a single sensation you'll call "Being Balanced" and shift into long term memory. This improves your chances of hitting that position, correctly and consistently, during UnderSwitch, or ZipperSwitch. In each of those drills, you'll begin examining a whole new series of mini-skills, using the short-term memory you've just freed up for the job.

If it sounds complicated and challenging it is. That's why I urge you not to waste time on unexamined rote repeats, or activities like kicking that don't polish important details or create new connections. The secret to making the process manageable is a third phenomenon observed in expert learners and performers in fields from math to music to sports.

Anders Ericsson, a psychology professor at Florida State University, is the leading figure in the Expert Performance Movement, a group of scholars studying the question: When someone is very good at something, what is it that makes him good? Ericsson and his colleagues have studied expert performers in a range of pursuits, including soccer, golf, surgery, piano, Scrabble, chess, software design, stock picking and darts. They concluded that masterful performers in nearly any field are nearly always *made* through practice, not born.

For example, when they studied classical pianists, they found that winners of competitions had practiced over 10,000 hours by the age of 20, while runners up had practiced less than half as long. But does practice always make perfect? I.E. How do you explain the dominance of a Tiger Woods or Roger Federer, when dozens of other golf or tennis pros also spend endless hours practicing? Ericsson found the difference when he compared *how* both groups practice.

Expert performers shun mindless drills and rote repetition for what he called Deliberate Practice. They set specific goals, continuously analyze their progress and focus on *process* not outcomes. In swimming that means focus on the *feel* of your stroke before you focus on stroke count – and on both feel and count, before you focus on time. "A crucial part of practicing well is that you are always learning," Ericsson says. "Expert performers constantly find ways to integrate learning into the doing."

The final difference between expert performers and "average performers" in all fields can be summed up in the phrase "Don't let the good become the enemy of the great." While average performers often became satisfied with what they achieved, expert performers are *never* satisfied. They always feel they can improve. So Expert Performers are Kaizen Performers as well.

Time to Swim

Now that you understand the fundamentals of Effective Training, and how to learn skills with the best, let's take our training to the pool. The Breaststroke and Backstroke chapters contained brief sections on how to practice those strokes as you develop them. The Butterfly and Freestyle chapters included more detail. In the next three chapters I'll augment the information I've already provided in many places throughout the book by expanding on the three phases of stroke development outlined in the Freestyle chapter.

EFFECTIVE TRAINING PHASE ONE

Develop Comfort and Self-Awareness

Your main goal, in this phase, is to develop an "aquatic brain." Your "land brain" is expert at managing balance and movement when you are stable, subject to gravity and vertical. Your aquatic brain must learn to manage your body when you are unstable, subject to resistance and horizontal. Until you overcome the UHSP tendencies (described in Chapter 2) that have limited your efficiency, whole-stroke swimming may reinforce those habits and delay improvement. Thus the best way to break "struggling habits" is to replace some of your whole-stroke laps with TI drills.

Use your first few practices to explore the first couple of drills for each stroke with a sense of curiosity, and no self-imposed pressure to complete a certain distance or move at a given speed. Any time you feel even minor discomfort during a drill, your natural reaction will be some form of struggle, which will imprint in your muscle memory. Thus ease and patience is essential.

In his martial arts "bible," *Tao of Jeet Kune Do*, martial arts legend Bruce Lee wrote that critical skills should always be practiced when your muscles are fresh. (He also wrote "ten minutes of practice with mind and body fully integrated is worth more than 10 hours of going through the motions.") Patience in mastering basic skills may be natural to martial artists and dancers, but not to most swimmers. So a good guideline for your first 10 to 20 hours of TI Practice is to learn to make mindful, examined movement a habit. Don't count laps or watch the pace clock. Focus on the key points detailed in the drill chapters and on reducing effort and increasing flow.

Your concentrated drill practice may last a few weeks to several months. The four stroke chapters include dozens of specific instructions and tips. Before any practice session, review those you intend to work on.

A Guide to Drill Practice

The grooming of an elite swimmer usually begins at age 7 or 8 and continues for 10 or more years of swimming up to 2000 miles per year. In other words an Olympic medallist may have swum the equivalent of *eight times around the world* since taking up the sport. This is so, in part, because as I noted, swimming well isn't natural to humans.

If it takes that much training to produce an Olympian, what are the rest of us – often without professional guidance and with far fewer hours to invest – to do? Stroke drills are the quickest and most effective way to master swimming skills. Because TI drills are so easy to learn, even inexperienced swimmers can use them effectively for self-coaching.

Drills streamline the process by which elite swimmers achieve their striking flow: While training they occasionally experience moments when something feels just right, moments they intuitively store in a mental catalogue of similar experiences. Eventually, the catalogue becomes comprehensive enough to produce a highly efficient stroke. But among the reasons these swimmers cover such astounding mileage is because this process is often haphazard.

When your time is limited, trial-and-error is too inefficient a way to master an intricate skill. So we've choreographed a series of exercises intended to produce "snapshot sensations" like those élite swimmers feel. By following the steps outlined in the preceding chapters, you can create your own catalogue, and access these sensations in an orderly way, instead of by accident. When you resume swimming the whole stroke after polishing the parts in drills, your body should assemble them naturally into an ever-improving whole. Here are some tips for staying on course to a beautiful and efficient stroke:

Know the objective. When practicing any drill for the first time, use your initial repetitions to clarify the problem the drill is meant to solve, e.g. remaining comfortable as you lift your arm in a Backstroke recovery. Follow that with repetitions dedicated to working out the solution. Then complete the process by "memorizing" that solution until it comes naturally. Then use that new mini-skill to address the next problem – of which one drill may have three or more, each requiring the same problem-solving approach.

First think, then feel. Reading this book will improve your *intellectual* understanding of how human bodies behave in the water. To swim well, you need to know "in your bones" how your body behaves in the water. To develop this mind-muscle connection, explore every new drill with curiosity and patience. Experiment to learn what happens when you alter new movements even slightly. Every experience – even those that feel wrong – will move you closer to being guided by sensation rather than thought, freeing brainpower for the next problem.

Breathe. While learning a new drill, devote at least a few repetitions in each set to breathing awareness. Breath holding may occur involuntarily when concentrating on a challenging movement, leading to muscle tension and loss of flow. Bubble out steadily and quietly, especially if you can't inhale immediately. (Bubbling from your nose will improve breath control.) And "cleansing breaths" – inhaling deep and slow, relaxing on the exhale – between reps, rather than watching the pace clock, will keep you fresh physically and alert mentally.

Keep it short. Drills build good skills only when they're done well. If you're not fresh – both physically and mentally – your practice will suffer. Your focus and movements will be most accurate when you practice repeats of 25 meters or less, then rest until you feel ready to repeat as well or better than last time. Focus on making each rep a little smoother and more relaxed, a little more precise and economical. If that's not happening, review the focal points, or return to the previous drill to strengthen your foundation.

It's the movements that matter. Focus on how you feel, not on distance or time. I ignore the pace clock, and even forgo counting laps during drill practice. You can segment your practice by focusing on a drill for, say 12 minutes, then move to your next task when 12 minutes is up…or stay with it if you feel a promising flow developing or a breakthrough coming.

Test your stroke. After working for 10 to 15 minutes on a new drill, try at least a length or two of whole stroke. What felt better in the drill? Can you feel more of that in your stroke? Can you swim each length a little easier? You won't undo your progress if your stroke is less than perfect as you compare sensations. Even moments of struggle, if you become more aware of its causes, can help move you toward the goal. But don't prolong that struggle beyond the time it takes you to sharpen your focus.

When you can swim with improved efficiency for several minutes nonstop – or repeat intervals of 50 to 100 meters for 10 to 15 minutes, you are probably ready to move to the next phase of practice – at least for that stroke or a particular aspect of that stroke. As you do, keep in mind that you will likely want to return to Phase One practice again and again, with higher goals or subtler objectives each time.

EFFECTIVE TRAINING PHASE TWO

Develop Your Stroke

In my early 40s, I won several medals at Masters National Championships and thought I was swimming about as well as possible. But 10 years later, as a result of having to limit my training while recovering from two surgeries and a cycling accident, I made completely unexpected breakthroughs. Months of being able to do only the simplest and gentlest of drills, followed by more months of slow, easy whole stroke, produced dramatic improvements in my Freestyle. In Phase Two, you'll train in a similar way as you transition from patient drill practice to *examined* whole stroke, not just imprinting new movements, but making constant self-monitoring a habit.

Your transition won't come by abruptly replacing drills with swimming. Instead, you'll make a gradual shift – doing a drill for 25 meters, then swimming for 50 (or 75 or 100) rather than for 25 meters as before, focused on maintaining a sensation the drill has made you more aware of. Over weeks and months, you'll slowly increase the percentage of whole-stroke in your total training.

As your technique improves, your opportunities for refinement come more from whole-stroke practice. While drills are best for highlighting and honing a particular aspect of technique – e.g. tipping your fingers down on the Freestyle catch – whole stroke is best for coordinating two or more aspects – e.g. keeping fingers down while breathing. But not "autopilot swimming." It takes focused *practice* to continue improving. The training modes outlined below bring organization and clear purpose to this form of training and help you make progress day by day.

E.G. While trying to imprint that patient, fingers-down catch while breathing in Freestyle, you'll succeed initially on a few short repeats, say 8 x 25 at very low speed. Next you'll aim to maintain it for a longer set of 25s or increase to 50s. Your goal will be increased consistency – keep fingers down and catch patiently on *every one* of the 32 strokes you might take in each 50. After you become "boringly consistent" with that habit, test how it holds up at higher speed. And it may take years for you to feel the same while *racing*.

And that process is for just one piece of coordination. When you turn your attention to linking leg drive with that fingers-down, patient catch, you repeat the same process, with a new focus or goal.

Now that I've explained how to transition from drills to whole-stroke practice, here are the general goals for all strokes in Phase Two:

- Swim with consistent relaxation.
- Swim in balance and with long, sleek bodylines.
- Breathe without compromising your body position, or the timing and coordination of your stroke.
- *Hold* water, rather than pull it.
- Be able to maintain a consistent SPL range of three to four 25-yd/mtr stroke counts for each stroke you're practicing.

Have you noticed no mention of time or speed? Phase Two is exclusively about consistent execution of effective strokes. While using the pace clock is not forbidden, it's a secondary priority. In Phase Two, our primary measuring tool will be stroke count, rather than time. Once you focus on the time it takes you to complete your repeats, you've begun transitioning to Phase Three.

Develop Your Stroke with Drill/Swim

Drills transform largely by providing powerful insights into what an efficient stroke feels like, as if you could do a "virtual lap" inside the skin of a skilled swimmer. In drill-swim sets, ask yourself "What feels different and better about this drill, compared to how swimming usually feels?" Then maintain that feeling for as long as you can while swimming whole stroke. When you lose it, resume drilling.

How many laps of drill and how many of swim? Drill until it feels just right; at first that may take 100 yards or more. Then continue swimming for as long as your stroke feels as good as the drill, at first that may be only 25 yards. As you get better at both, it may take only 50 yards of drill to feel just right and you may be able to swim feeling *that good* for the same distance. Ultimately, you'll find that it takes only a brief reminder, perhaps 25 yards of drill, to nail that feeling and you can sustain it while swimming for three or more lengths.

With continued practice, you should be able to swim even farther with that feeling. By then you may have shifted your attention to a new focal point for that drill, or to the next drill in the sequence. The proportion of drill to swim can change from day to day or drill to drill. If you're feeling a bit more tired or a bit less smooth, do more drills. If you feel sharp and fresh, swim more. But keep in mind that musicians good enough to play at Carnegie Hall still practice their scales every day. The only "rule" for your transition to whole stroke is "Never Practice Struggle."

Hone your Stroke with Mindful Swimming

When you feel ready to leave the drills out of some of your drill-swim sets, simply continue concentrating on the same sensations – to the exclusion of virtually anything else you might think about. When heightened awareness of a highly specific part of your stroke – rather than distance, time or speed – is your core goal during a set, you're doing Mindful Swimming. Here's how it works:

If you've swum Freestyle for several years with an inefficient wide-swinging recovery, that's become deeply embedded in your long-term memory and it takes a concerted effort to dislodge it. Begin that process in Phase One by practicing ZipperSwitch drills and continue it in Phase Two by swimming with a "Marionette Arms" focus.

At first the new recovery will feel odd, and the moment you stop thinking intently about it you'll probably swing wider again. But each lap you consciously focus on Marionette Arms makes a relaxed and compact recovery a bit more natural. After 15 minutes thinking only about that you'll improve the chances that you'll keep doing it when you're *not* thinking about it. Each time you devote another 15 minutes to it, it becomes a bit more permanent.

If you systematically practice the focal points mentioned in each stroke chapter, the complex challenge of building a really efficient stroke becomes a more manageable – and enjoyable – task. With each passing hour, week, and month of purposeful practice, each piece will be polished independently and fit a bit more naturally with the other pieces, while you avoid feeling overwhelmed by complexity.

How long will it take until your new stroke is perfect and permanent? The rest of your life! You can continue improving endlessly. But my rule of thumb for transforming a skill into a "no-brainer" – i.e. you do it even when you're not thinking about it – is 50,000 meters. Not that you should think only about Marionette Arms for the next 2000 laps, but after you *have* devoted 50,000 meters to that focus, over a period of two to three years, it should be deeply embedded in long-term memory.

Practice Mindful Swimming

As when you become acquainted with a new drill, start using each new Focal Point by concentrating on it for 15 or more minutes, before shifting to another focus. As that Focal Point feels more natural, alternate it with others with gradually increasing frequency. Here's an example of a Mindful Swimming series incorporating three focal points that will make your Freestyle recovery/entry relaxed and efficient:

Block Practice

300 yards of Marionette Arms + 300 yards of Ear Hops + 300 yards of Mail Slot.

Several weeks later: Random Practice

3 rounds of: (100 yards of Marionette Arms + 100 yards of Ear Hops + 100 yards of Mail Slot).

Several months later: Very Random Practice

12 x 75 as: (25 yards of Marionette Arms + 25 yards of Ear Hops + 25 yards of Mail Slot).

Block practice is best when the focal point is less familiar. Staying with it longer allows you to tweak it and heighten your awareness of small variations. As that sensation and pattern move into long-term memory, your brain can process new tasks more frequently. Changing tasks more frequently is one of the best ways to accelerate the shift from short-term to long-term memory and "automaticity." However if you try to advance from block to random too quickly, you run the risk of imprinting a ragged habit.

Mindfulness in Open-Water

One of the best places to practice Focal Points is with purposeful open-water practice. A drawback of doing Mindful Swimming in a pool is this experience: You push off and begin working on Marionette Arms. After 10 or 12 strokes you start to become attuned to what your arms do in that fleeting moment between exit and entry. Then the wall interrupts your concentration and you have to start all over. Just as you begin to feel it, you lose the flow. So a 50-meter pool is better than a 25-yard pool and best of all is a course that's even longer – i.e., a calm lake, reservoir or cove.

In open water, you can "groove" that sensation then continue imprinting for a hundred or more unbroken strokes. And considering that open water seldom offers a pace clock, practicing Focal Points, for a set number of strokes is a good way to bring structure to an open water swim.

Stroke Counting

A key difference between TI training and conventional workouts is constant awareness of Stroke Length. In Mindful Swimming sets, you should occasionally count strokes to compare the efficiency of various Focal Points, then gradually make SPL the main focus of some of certain sets. This means: (1) count your strokes, and (2) maintain an efficient count for greater distances, or reduce your count at shorter distances. You probably won't succeed every time in hitting your target count, but even when you miss, you'll become more aware of why you lose efficiency.

Learn your Stroke Length

Whenever you're not doing a drill or Mindful Swimming, count your strokes – every stroke, every lap. This will give you real-time info on your efficiency. How much does your count increase when you swim 50s at 45 seconds, rather than 48 seconds, or when you swim 100-yard repeats, rather than 50s. Then begin setting efficiency goals for every length of practice. Those goals are not strictly about taking fewer strokes. They can also include:

1. Reducing the increase that occurs when you swim faster.
2. Reducing the increase that occurs when you swim farther.

Consolidate Your Stroke Length

Once you have awareness of your stroke count range, use that knowledge in sets that increase your ability to stay efficient for greater distances. A simple way is with ladder sets in which each repeat is longer than the one before it. Here are several examples:

Swim 3 to 4 rounds of: 25+50+75+100. Rest for 3 to 5 "cleansing breaths" between repeats and for a minute or two between rounds. Your goal is to minimize the SPL increase that occurs as you progress from the 25 to the 100. Can you do a better job of keeping your SPL constant on the later rounds than you did on the early rounds?

Swim 1 to 3 rounds of: 50+100+150+200. Rest for 4 to 6 breaths between repeats and 2 to 3 minutes between rounds.

This doubles the distance of the previous set. Do the shorter repeats at a *moderately* challenging SPL, then see how close you can stay to the initial SPL as the repeat distance increases. When you've progressed repeats of 200 or more meters with fairly consistent SPL, you can drop your count by 1SPL and start the process over again with 25- or 50-meter repeats. Your speed on these repeats is less important than a sense of smooth, consistent stroking over longer distances.

To focus on increasing your speed, swim ladder sets in reverse:

Swim 1 to 3 rounds of: 200+150+100+50

Your goal is to hold your SPL from the 200 as the repeat distance decreases. If you were at 16SPL on the 200, you should find you can effortlessly swim faster at this SPL on the 100 or 50, than you did for 200 or 150 on that stroke count. This will begin to teach you the best reason for establishing and maintaining a good Stroke Length: it becomes the basis for increasing speed with relatively little effort.

EFFECTIVE TRAINING PHASE THREE

Increase Mastery, Distance and Speed

In Phase Two, you focused on making your stroke efficient. In Phase Three, you'll work on swimming farther and faster with the least additional effort, making your stroke *adaptable*, by developing the following capabilities:

- Swim exactly the SPL you choose at any time.
- Swim faster when you raise your SPL.
- Comfortably maintain your SPL for longer distances.
- Use the pace clock to know the "efficiency cost" of swimming fast.

Phase Three Practice Tips

Phase Three is forever – *purposeful* training you can do for the rest of your life, no matter how accomplished you become. Here is a brief summary of how to modify forms of practice you used in Phases One and Two.

Drill Practice

Drills will be valuable for as long as you swim, but as time passes, you should learn more from advanced drills because they help you integrate the various parts of the stroke. You can still practice basic drills to address specific problems. In Backstroke, I notice water sloshing over my face when my left hand enters, which tells me my balance isn't quite as good at that moment. So I continue to practice the Streamline and Partial Lift drills with my left arm extended ahead of me to correct my imbalance. But I feel that Switch drills do the most to improve my speed. When you practice drills, alternate with whole-stroke laps to apply the lessons immediately.

The best times for drill practice in a training session are:

- **Warmup** – Because you learn best when mind and muscles are fresh.
- **Preset** – A brief drill set will prime your muscles for efficiency during your Main Set.
- **Postset** – Gently paced Drills will help you recover faster after an intense effort while helping you regain any lost efficiency.
- **Do the UnKick** – If you swim with a team and can do so, practice drills when everyone else grabs kickboards.

Mindful Swimming

As you gain in skill and experience, choose focal points that solve specific problems, as I suggested for your drill practice. My main Freestyle focus for the first five months of this year was to hold water more firmly with my right hand, while breathing to my left. For the past four months, it has been to integrate my leg drive and hand-spear.

Though I've been swimming the other strokes for decades, my understanding of them has changed so much of late, that I'm in Phase Two Practice with them…and might be for several years. Thus I divide my attention among several focal points in Butterfly, Backstroke and Breaststroke.

The best times to include Mindful Swimming in a training session are:

- **Warmup** – For the same reason you might do drills here.
- **Preset** – If you did drills in your warmup, Focal Points are a logical transition to your main set.
- **Main Set** – Why not do *examined swimming* on your main

set? I always do. If the main set is more speed-oriented, I use it to test my ability to maintain a technique I've been imprinting in slower sets. If it's longer, and more moderately paced, I demand more technical precision of myself.

- **Postset** – For the same reason you might do drills here.

Stroke Counting

In Phase Three, you'll focus less on reducing your SPL and more on being able to swim a variety of stroke counts and on being able to stay efficient and gain measurable speed when you add a stroke or two per length.

If you began counting strokes regularly in Phase Two, you may have wondered if your stroke count is right for you. An optimal stroke count – the one that has the lowest energy cost for any distance or speed – is fairly individual. So here's a formula, based on arm length and the distance of your typical pushoff that allows you to predict your own personal "highly efficient" stroke count for Freestyle – the one you should aim for when swimming short distances at low speed. You can allow 2 to 3 additional SPL for higher speeds.

For a 25-yard pool: High Efficiency SPL = $12 \times (L\text{-}P)/A$.
For a 25-meter pool: High Efficiency SPL = $(L\text{-}P)/A$

SPL = strokes per length
L = Length of pool (in feet or meters)
P = distance traveled in pushoff before stroking (in feet or meters)
A = Armspan from wrist to wrist (in inches or meters)

I'm 6'-0" tall with a 57-inch wingspan and I usually surface after pushoff at the 15-foot mark in a 75-foot pool, so according to this formula it should take me 12.6 high efficiency strokes to cover the remaining 60 feet (20 yards.) And in fact, when I practice low speed, high mindfulness swimming I take 12 to 13 strokes. When I swim faster I take 14 to 15 strokes, which is also the count at which I try to race. My Backstroke SPL is about one stroke above my Freestyle. My Breaststroke SPL is about half my Backstroke count and my Butterfly SPL is about one stroke above my Breaststroke.

Remember, as I said in Chapter 5, your high efficiency SPL – the lowest count you typically use – should be fluid, effortless, and silent. If you find yourself unable to swim the count predicted by the formula above, don't strain to reach it. Instead, patiently continue with your drills and Mindful Swimming, until your efficiency allows you to swim the predicted SPL with a relaxed, leisurely – but still rhythmic – stroke.

Add **Strokes to your SPL**

If this sounds like I'm suggesting you give up your hard-won efficiency, I'm not. When you achieve the high efficiency SPL described above, you have a stroke count that's ideal for disciplined, thoughtful practice that builds aerobic conditioning and good habits at the same time. To convert efficiency into speed, you'll practice swimming *efficiently* at higher stroke counts, not wheel-spinning. Our training is designed to ensure that a higher SPL is a *choice* and not an accident, and that it makes you *faster*, not just tired.

Think of this kind of training as intended to give you swimming *gears* like those you use to ride a bicycle or drive a car. Your high efficiency SPL (let's call it "N") is 1st gear. Add a stroke (N+1) and you're in 2nd gear. Add another stroke (N+2) for 3rd gear. That should be sufficient, in a 25 yard/meter pool, for most swimmers new to this kind of practice. As your skill increases, you'll probably be able to add a 4th gear in Freestyle and perhaps in Backstroke.

You should practice using these gears with sets that, at times, will be similar to a piano student playing scales until she becomes deft in striking the right keys every time. You'll want to develop just as much facility in changing your SPL lap by lap.

Your goals with these exercises include: (1) learn to swim smoothly and effectively at every count in your range, (2) be able to "calibrate" your stroke so you can swim at any count you choose in your range at any time, and (3) increase speed with far less effort by smoothly increasing your stroke count.

Sample Sets to Develop Swimming Gears

Here are several "starter sets" to begin exploring your ability to change your SPL at will. Advanced swimmers can double the distance of each repeat.

Swim 25+50+75+100. Rest for 3 to 5 cleansing breaths after each swim.

Count your strokes on the 25, then swim at a consistent pace or effort on the other swims and see what happens to your SPL average. If you took 15 strokes for the 25, your stroke count will probably go above 30-45-60 on the 50-75-100. How much change is there? Next time you swim the set, can you increase by fewer strokes? File that information for future reference.

Swim 100+75+50+25. Rest for 3 to 5 breaths after each swim.

Start with an easy 100. Count your strokes and divide by 4. This number becomes your "N" (benchmark spl) for the rest of the set. E.G., If you took 72 strokes, your N is 18 SPL (72 divided by 4 lengths). Note how far below 54-36-18 strokes you are for 75-50-25.

Swim 25+50+75+100. Rest for 3 to 5 breaths after each swim.

Repeat this set with a specific focal point – e.g. patient hands or swimming more quietly – to learn how that affects your efficiency, most importantly as the distance increases.

Swim 4 to 6 rounds of 3 x 25. Rest for 3 to 5 breaths between swims and 30 seconds between rounds.

1st Round: @   N-N+1-N+2
2nd Round: @   N+2-N+1-N
3rd Round: @   N-N+1-N+2
4th Round: @   N+2-N+1-N

On the first two rounds just calibrate your SPL, testing how accurately you can adjust your timing to hit the wall in exactly the prescribed count. The puzzle of subtracting strokes (2nd Round) will turn out to be a completely different task than that of adding strokes. On the next two rounds, see how fast you can swim at each stroke count. When putting more emphasis on speed: (1) Just feel it, don't time it; and (2) Take as much rest as you want.

Swim 2 to 4 rounds of 3 x 50. Rest for 5 breaths between 50s and 30-60 seconds between rounds.

1st Round: 25@N-25@N+1
2nd Round: 25@N+1-25@N+2
3rd Round: 25@N+2-25@N+3

When you first practice this set, just get comfortable with hitting the prescribed count on each length. The second step is to stay smooth and fluent at every stroke count. Do as many rounds as you want, as long as it feels good and remains interesting. Experiment with Focal Points, staying with one for a full round or longer. You can also break up the set by doing 100 to 200 yards of your favorite drills between rounds. (When you become truly effortless on this, you won't need any extra rest between rounds.) For progression, move up to 75-yard repeats with counts of N, N+1, N+2 on one and N+1, N+2, N+3 on the next.

Your goal is to practice sets like these, mindfully and patiently, until you can practically do them in your sleep and smoothly hit any stroke count you choose, while feeling controlled and fluent at all times.

Finally, if you find all of this almost boringly easy, here's a challenge that is guaranteed to put your SPL adaptability to a severe test. Do the 50s or 75s in reverse order. In other words, like this: 25@N+2, 25@N+1, 25@N

Swim Golf

Until now, we've suggested you focus exclusively on developing movement quality and adaptive stroke length. The final piece of your Stroke Development process is to begin using the pace clock as another piece of information – in addition to sensation and SPL – to measure how effectively you're swimming. But as you do, it's essential to maintain the efficiency you've focused on up to now. The best tool for doing so is Swim Golf.

To play Swim Golf, count your strokes for 25 or 50 yards or meters, and add your time in seconds to get your Score. Playing Swim Golf and experimenting with a variety of combinations of SPL and time helps you learn how to achieve the greatest speeds with the greatest efficiency.

Ways to play include:

1. Swim 3-4 x 50. Swim each at the same time, but try to reduce your count by one stroke per 50.

2. Swim 3-4 x 50. Swim each at the same count, but try to reduce your time.

3. Swim a series of 50s to achieve a best or average score, then practice your favorite drill, and repeat the series to see if you can improve your score.

4. Swim a series of 50s with one focal point to achieve a best or average score, then repeat with a different focal point and compare your results.

5. Add 3 to 5 to your personal best score for a particular stroke, and see how long you can maintain that score for a longer set of 50s or a set on shorter rest. For instance, my best score for 50 yards of Freestyle is 57. So I sometimes test my ability to repeat 50s at a score of 60, 61, or 62.

6. Mix two strokes. E.G. What's your score for 50s of 25 Fly + 25 Backstroke? Or 25 Backstroke + 25 Breaststroke?

This completes our lifetime swimming-improvement program for developing your strokes, and enriching your swimming experience. While we have not covered the physical conditioning aspects of training, you should now be able to effectively develop your strokes to a high level. If you follow this method faithfully, we promise you'll improve your endurance, speed, and fitness. While there are additional ways to train, these forms of practice should keep most any swimmer productively engaged for years. While you get started with stroke development, we'll begin work on a book and internet services that offers more detail on training the neuromuscular and aerobic systems.

Share the Love!

My purpose in writing this book is to share my love of swimming with you. I'm fortunate to have many people that share my love for swimming, some on-line at the TI Discussion Forum (www.totalimmersion.net/talk-back. html) and others I swim with regularly. One of the best things you can do for your own swimming is to build a small "community" of other swimmers who feel the same way and have similar goals. Some things you can do:

1) Visit the Find a TI Buddy conference on the TI Discussion Forum.

2) Wear a TI cap or other apparel at the pool, as you practice. Swimmers who find your grace appealing - or are simply made curious - will ask what you're doing.

3) With management's permission, post a notice at your pool asking if other swimmers there are interested in TI practice.

4) Teach some basics to a friend, family member or new TI buddy. In teaching even the most basic parts of what you're learning to someone else, you clarify your own concepts to a greater degree than is possible any other way (short of receiving direct instruction from a certified TI coach.)

Visit www.totalimmersion.net/share.html to learn how to teach simple TI.

Resources

The Total Immersion Web Site: www.totalimmersion.net

The Total Immersion Web site will be a priceless source of no-charge support and information. Important features include:

- *Total Swim*, a free newsletter featuring invaluable useful articles published 10 times a year. A key ingredient of *Total Swim* is articles contributed by TI students like you, sharing the insights that have helped them reach their goals. Please consider becoming a contributor.

- An on-line Discussion Forum for swimmers who are using this book and TI methods to improve their swimming. Use the Discussion Forum to share your insights, discoveries, and successes, to ask questions and to tap the experience of others who are on the same path as you.

- Video clips spotlighting key refinements of TI drills and skills.

- Samples of TI-specific practices for both technique improvement and effective training.

- A directory of trained and certified TI Coaches available to work with you toward achievement of your goals and complete swimming fulfillment.

Masters Swimming Websites for the US and Canada

www. usms.org and www.mymsc.ca

"Masters" swimming doesn't mean elite or deadly serious. Masters swimmers are people much like you, who belong to groups organized in nearly every country to provide coached workouts, competitions, clinics and workshops for adults aged 18 and over. These programs welcome all adult swimmers – fitness, triathlete, competitive, non-competitive – who are dedicated to improving their fitness through swimming.

These are the web sites for Masters Swimming in the US and Canada. They provide information on joining Masters swimming, links to Masters clubs in your area and to Masters Swimming organizations in other countries around the world. You can also find a calendar of pool, open-water, and postal swimming events and a directory of thousands of places to swim.

Total Immersion Self-Help Tools

If this book has piqued your interest in developing yourself further as a swimmer, TI offers books and DVDs that distill the complex movements of swimming into simple concepts and progressions that can help *any* swimmer achieve satisfaction and maximize their potential. TI books and videos are fully guaranteed to be the best swim-improvement tools available. For complete information, visit www.totalimmersion.net or call 800-609-7946 or 845-256-9770.

TOTAL IMMERSION DVDs

Happy Laps: Total Immersion for Beginners

If you're a non-swimmer…if you can swim only a few strokes…if you're intimidated by deep water, this is the TI DVD for you. Illustrates a simple, clear, common-sense approach for learning to be completely at home in the water, experiencing flow, ease and real joy – in just a few hours – with a combination of partnered and self-guided "discovery exercises." Lesson One will teach you to be completely comfortable in the water and how to breathe comfortably. Lesson Two teaches you how your body naturally behaves in the water. Lesson Three will teach you to move through the water as fish do, with balanced, *slippery*, whole body movement. $29.95

Freestyle Made Easy

This 45-minute DVD illustrates the TI Freestyle lesson sequence with each step examined from above and below water, and in slow motion and stop action. It also includes instruction in breathing, open water swimming and turns, both the relaxing open turn and the fast flip turn. $39.95

Butterfly for Every Body
Backstroke for Every Body
Breaststroke for Every Body

Where most swim technique videos feature lavishly gifted elite swimmers, our DVDs show "average" swimmers – Terry Laughlin and other TI coaches – who have achieved Extraordinary efficiency and grace using the TI method. This series of three DVDS has been produced expressly to complement the written descriptions and photos in the Strokes section of this book. Each stroke is presented via a "live" lesson, featuring Terry Laughlin showing how he learned to swim that stroke efficiently, complemented by slow motion and stop-action surface and underwater views. See samples at www.totalimmersion.net. $29.95

TOTAL IMMERSION BOOKS ·····················

Freestyle Made Easy Drill Cards The next best thing to having your own TI coach at the pool. Our waterproof Drill Cards illustrate every step from our Freestyle Made Easy DVD with every key point illustrated by surface and underwater photo's. $29.95

Triathlon Swimming Made Easy: How ANYONE Can Succeed in Triathlon or Open Water Swimming

If you think you'd like to venture out from the pool to tackle a triathlon or try your hand at Open Water swimming, TSME provides a step-by-step learning plan that will help you swim with ease and confidence for any distance in any body of water. $24.95

Here are some simple tips for Sharing the Love with another swimmer:

1. "Hang" Your Head

- Head-spine alignment is essential to efficient swimming.

- Release your head's weight and look directly down, not forward.

2. Lengthen Your Body

- A longer body line moves through the water faster and easier.

- Focus on using arms to lengthen your body line (rather than push water back.)

- Slip your arm into the water as if sliding it into a mail slot.

3. Move like Water

- Smooth strokes are more effective than splashy ones.

- Never "practice struggle." Swim as quietly as possible.

4. Count your Strokes

- Stroke count is your simplest measure of efficiency.

- Try any of the preceding three points and see how it affects your stroke count.

Happy Laps!